Trouble So Hard

Labor and Life in the African-American Community
Eden Town, NC
1870 - 1900

Audrey Jean Sapp Childs

Trouble So Hard

Labor and Life
in the
African-American Community

Edenton Town, North Carolina

1870–1900

Audrey Jean Sapp Childs

HERITAGE BOOKS
2017

HERITAGE BOOKS

AN IMPRINT OF HERITAGE BOOKS, INC.

Books, CDs, and more—Worldwide

For our listing of thousands of titles see our website
at
www.HeritageBooks.com

Published 2017 by
HERITAGE BOOKS, INC.
Publishing Division
5810 Ruatan Street
Berwyn Heights, Md. 20740

International Standard Book Number
Paperbound: 978-0-7884-5793-7

Dedication to the Ancestors

Coming from a powerful line of people who have shared stories, danced and sung sacred songs about their struggles and victories for centuries, I honor and embody the essence of my ancestors. From the time of our spiritual existence until now, there have always been a few that have been chosen, a few that have been called to be the voice of the forgotten souls of yesterday. Through their deeds and determination, they take on tasks to unravel and reveal the ambiguities of who our ancestors were, so that we can gain a sense of who we are as a people.

"Trouble So Hard" is an authentic example of such tasks, as it offers words to those driven by evidence of things felt but unseen, providing a gateway for those who are searching for a piece of themselves from a long-ago time. It is about reverencing our ancestors while connecting to our history, our culture, our possibilities, and our achievements. "Trouble So Hard" will give you a spark to walk in the significance of you ancestors' shadows as an extension of their legacy for the 21st century and beyond.

Divinely intertwined as a result of the existence of our ancestors, and like the woven strips of the vibrant Kente cloth of royalty, we are held together with stitches of honor, respect, and love. Place your hands on your chest as you breathe deeply, and listen carefully to the rhythm of your heartbeat. This is the vibrational essence of your ancestors' whispers reminding you that our presence is a gift to be cherished forever. Everyone has a story and this one is about providing you with hope and inspiration to journey on a path that is before us all to stand tall, as one in the struggle to obtain and maintain a sense of spiritual equity for our beloved ancestors.

Towards Enlightenment,

Dr. Kim D. Harris

Thank you...to all of my Facebook friends and family who cheered me on, every time I posted about the progress of the book, over many years and months.

Thank you...to my dear friend Debra Strickland and her daughter Binahkaye Joy for the picture that hangs in my study, and the sentiment behind it that kept me encouraged, pushing and wondering about what is always, "just around the bend..."

Contents

Foreword

Preface

Articles Found in *Fisherman and Farmer*

Part One

Part Two

Articles from *Fisherman and Farmer*

"Oh Lordy, trouble so hard, Oh Lordy, trouble so hard.

Don't nobody know my troubles but God,

Don't nobody know my troubles but God."

Foreword

Robert James Childs

The black American has traveled a long and interesting road. The history of Blacks in the United States originates before the country was even known as such! We are descendants of those who have seen the birth of the United States of America through all of its tumultuous ups and downs, from when humans were property; to when humans banded together under a common cause and defeated a threat to humanity, under the guise of a government. Black Americans have been a strong, colorful, and lengthy thread in the tapestry that makes up the United States.

When examining the history of the black American, we find that even though the experience has been difficult most of the time, almost every generation has found a way to rise. Upon this examination, we see a population of people intentionally and systematically stripped of their original culture, then forced to practice customs of a foreign land. Through the circumstances, we detect the resilience of these forced immigrants. Not only did they leave their own customs, but they also created and built their own culture , using what survived the journey from the homeland, what was forced on them, and what was newly created while in the United States. For example, they patched together oral traditions and paired them with songs they hear in the United States, creating what we know now as spirituals and later, gospel music. When you sprinkle some artful expression into that, you get the beginnings of what we know as jazz. These two examples are just two of many was the black American has colorfully contributed to the United States' tapestry.

On the other side, the United States has occasionally and reluctantly accepted what Black America was offering, neglecting to include the populations into American culture. Many times, black Americans were told to "go back where (they) came from", that they weren't wanted in some sections of the country, and that they weren't worth as much as other Americans. But this warranted questions such as "Where are we supposed to go?" Certain people who don't see blacks as equals, or who would rather see blacks "go back where they came from", don't recognize that the Black American has been present since before the Revolutionary War. Black Americans created their own culture after they were brought from another continent. Black Americans created their own economy when they were no longer used as tools for free labor.

Decades later, Black Americans chanted "Say it loud, I'm black and I'm proud!", when they were told they were worthless. They chanted "black is beautiful", when they were told they were ugly. The Black American spoke truth to power when an authoritarian government seemed to have forgotten them. Black Americans will be here to grow and evolve along with the United States. Over the course of history, it hasn't been perfect, but black America always finds a way to survive and thrive.

Dedication
Glenn Martin Childs

This book is dedicated to the ancestors, the catalysts, and the architects of the cornerstone. It is dedicated to those who chose to plant seeds for the future, knowing they would never taste the fruits of their labor. I have always viewed life itself to be the single greatest gift of all. The bounty of joys and pleasures I have experienced in my short time could never be tainted by the evils which some find essential for their being.

When I began to have a clear understanding of all it took just for me to exist, when I began to learn how to weigh the amount of history which flows through our blood; and when I began to see how that history has intricately stitched together the DNA of the millions of ancestors to produce the gift that has been given to me, that is when I truly appreciated how those before me were able to *"Trouble So Hard."*

I have no memories of my mother's study ever being absent of some sort of information about our ancestry. I must admit to enjoying her lengthy but informative "come here real quick" conversations when she has a new lead or when her research had begun to pay off. I also must admit, that as a child I enjoyed watching her take long hours to spin through microfilm at the National Archives. It looked like fun, although I hated we couldn't play with the machines. Storytellers are necessary. They keep track of what was, so we may have a better understanding of what is, in hopes of improving what can be. It has been wonderful to watch my mother blossom and grow through the process of becoming an author and a storyteller in her own right.

"Trouble So Hard"

Labor and Life in the African-American Community in Edenton Town, NC

Preface

I am a descendant of slaves who made it through to see freedom, in the small town of Edenton, NC. Provey Cox and Betty Cox were slaves, at one time "belonging" to John Cox. John Cox was the owner of a brickyard and shipyard. He was also a railroad promoter, and operated an agricultural warehouse. Through years of research, I found that Cox obtained Provey in a sale across family lines, from his wife's side. The standard convention was that, usually, favored slaves were kept in the family, and not sold out. Cox's second wife, Ann Booth Pollock Clark, was the daughter of Hester Ann Buncombe and John Clark. Hester, along with her brother Thomas, and her sister Elizabeth Taylor, were the children of Colonel Edward Buncombe. Elizabeth married John Goelet, and they had three children; John, Eliza and Edward. Eliza married Thomas Benbury Haughton. When Thomas died in 1832 his brother, Charles Haughton was in charge of his estate. Among his estate were two slaves, Providence (Provey), sold to John Cox for $502, and Betty, sold to Thomas C. Whedbee, for $270. Through their mother's line, Eliza A.P. Goelet and Ann Booth Pollock Clark were first cousins, and the granddaughters of Edward Buncombe.

I haven't determined yet how Betty came to the Haughton family. However, I found Provey and Betty as married in 1831, in Barnetta McGhee White's work, "Somebody Knows My Name: Marriages of Freed People in North Carolina County by County". That tells me that they were recognized as being together one year before they were sold to separate owners.

At some point, Provey and Betty were reunited in the Cox household. I am still looking for a bill of sale from Whedbee to Cox. When John Cox died in 1856, Provey was purchased by Tristrim Lowther Skinner. The years between Skinner's purchase, and his death in a Civil War battle in 1862, are a span of time that I have not yet been able to document. In 1861, Provey's wife and children were petitioned for in the court in a division of slaves, by Cox's granddaughter, Eleanor, and her husband John C. Page. Page may have sought refuge in Virginia during the Civil War.

By 1866, Provey and Betty were reunited once again, and registered their marriage at the Chowan County courthouse, for a fee of .25, a substantial investment for a freedman. In 1867, Provey even registered to vote! In 1870 their son Harry, my great-great grandfather, married my great-great grandmother, Priscilla Blount, and for the first time, in the 1870 census, Provey and Betty were listed as people, and not a tally mark in a slave owner's column.

My goal is not to tell my family's story here, but to focus on what life in Edenton Town meant for hundreds of African Americans, upon whose backs Edenton was built. I found a disturbing quote in the guide map "African American Life in Edenton 1700's to the Present"- "One need look no further than the life of Harriet Jacobs, the former Edenton slave, author and abolitionist; and Golden Frinks, one of North Carolina's most important civil rights leaders to understand the importance of Edenton's African American history." I beg to differ. There are many more African Americans who did not rise to the ranks of popular and local recognition, as did Jacobs and Frinks. Their names will never be listed in an African American "Who's Who". They were the everyday workers and laborers; farm, field and factory hands. They were the nurses and cooks, the fishermen and carpenters who helped build Edenton for all of its residents, black and white.

It is for them, that I looked into history, into census records and lists of occupations, and created what I hope will be a statement that tells everyone who reads this, that we were there. Another note—two of the people whose names I found in the 1870 census appeared in the "Colored News" section in later copies of the Fisherman and Farmer, Edenton's newspaper at the time. So that you can read more about these people, I have placed an asterisk and a number beside their name. That number corresponds to articles that have been included in this book, following each name. I have done the same with people from the 1880 and 1900 censuses. Surnames are in bold type if they are in a list, with last names first. In the case of the historical narratives, if there are just a few names, I have put their names in regular order, for a better flow of reading.

I spent many years creating this, and I want to acknowledge the important people who helped me. First, my parents James and Lorraine Sapp, who instilled a love of reading and the pursuit of knowledge on all of my levels of education. My sisters Joan and Jacqueline have always supported my efforts in all I have done, and they have often offered resources that I could make use of. Both of them have taken trips to Edenton with me, looking at courthouse records, and even going to the grounds of Albania, the final home of John Cox, where my ancestors probably lived and worked. The cover design was created by Joan, and my daughter Regina. My children, Robert and his wife Laurine; Glenn, and Regina, have all been witness to my late nights at my computer. I am grateful to my cousins Odessa and Renee, who are also descendants of Provey and Betty. They have both taken time out of their schedules over the years to travel down Route 17 from Norfolk, to Edenton. They have also looked for records at the courthouse and library, and walked around both Vine Oak Cemetery and the African American Cemetery; understanding that they are both the final resting place for ancestors known and unknown. Each time we go, and although the route is much modernized, I know what lies deep on the other side of that road. I can imagine what the Dismal Swamp meant to hundreds of thousands of escaping slaves as they made their way North. I want to thank a cousin, Dr. Cynthia E. Harris, for making sure that my references were correctly cited, and an Edenton cousin, Dr. Kim Harris, for writing a heartfelt dedication to the ancestors.

Sometimes I think I missed out on the best parts of being a family historian because when my grandparents were still with us, family research hadn't become a phenomenon, and I didn't know the questions to ask because I was still young. I paid little attention to any conversations my parents may have had, about ancestors. Then along came Alex Haley's "Roots", and all of a sudden, the possibility for going deeper was born. The internet was invented, genealogy websites were created, and more and more people began to use the resources at the National Archives and the Church of Latter Day Saints. I was entranced, spending many days and nights at those institutions. I remember saying in a whispered, awestruck voice, "There you are...!" when the names of Provey and Betty were finally revealed to me on a roll of microfilmed bill of sale from a county deed book. I interviewed my great aunt, and though she was a child, and didn't remember too much about Edenton, she shared lots of stories about "Poppa", her father. Poppa was the grandson of Provey Cox, and the son of Provey's oldest child, Harry. Harry was born into slavery, and lived long enough to tell some of his children about it. My mother did tell me that once she had a school assignment, to ask a family member about slavery. She asked her grandfather, "Poppa". His response? "You don't want to know nuthin' 'bout that, sistah." He would speak no more on the topic. How telling....

Soon after that, I asked my mother if there were any family members left in Edenton, from whom I might get more information. She directed me to contact one cousin whom I'd never met. Her name was Beatrice Jones, and she lived on Gale Street. Through other connections, I was able to travel there, and began to meet people who helped me on my quest. I interviewed her, and have the tape of that interview today, even though she has since passed. One of those hot summer research days, I went to Shepard-Pruden Library. I met someone at that time, Mary Ann Coffey. She was doing some research on a topic of her own. Thinking she was the librarian, I asked her for help looking up resources the library may have had on the history of Edenton, specifically African American history there. I am eternally grateful to her, because she didn't just answer a few questions and send me on my way. She became a friend, and has, through the years, become my source of historical information, content and context for this book. She has sent me articles and books to read, prodded my thinking, and been a cheerleader for me, not only for the completion of this book, but for many of my life's circumstances. Facebook, which didn't exist when I started, has been the wonderful way for us to keep in touch.

Hopefully herein then, you will find the names of your ancestors. This book is meant to stir your imaginations, and encourage you to pursue your roots. Get started. It's a fascinating journey.

Articles Found in Fisherman and Farmer

The following articles provide more insight into the lives of some residents in Edenton Town whose identities are documented from the 1870, 1880 and 1900 censuses. Not everyone got his or her name in the paper, but each individual who went about making a way; working, conversing, praying, helping, raising a family, consuming, living and dying each day, contributed to the fabric of the town.

As you read, look for each name listed below. An article will immediately follow.

Readers are encouraged to read other selected articles in this volume. I tried to include articles about those who either worked in the various factories, or started up their own businesses that were patronized by both black and white residents. This list of course, is not exhaustive, and there are other sources still out there; perhaps some letters or documents or news articles can be found within your family.

*1. Gilliam, Atlas (wife Amie's death: *Fisherman and Farmer* 18 April 1890)

*2 Mayho, Edward (interesting article about how he died *Fisherman and Farmer 13 April, 1888)*

*3 Sutton, Edward (*Fisherman and Farmer 20 July 1888)*

*4 McGee, William (*Fisherman and Farmer 12 October 1888)*

*5 Skinner, Jacob (sold taffy and ice cream *Fisherman and Farmer* 3 June 1892)

*6 Leary, Sweety (*Fisherman and Farmer* 16 November 1888)

*7 James, Henry (*Fisherman and Farmer 7 October 1887*)

8 Tillery, Lewis/Louis(Fisherman and Farmer 22 April 1892; 6 January 1888)*

*9 Beasley, Henry (*Fisherman and Farmer 8 February 1889*)

*10 Lee, David (*Fisherman and Farmer 20 April 1888; 31 May 1889;1 August 1890; 27November 1891; 2 September 1892*)

*11 Dempsey, Emiline (*Fisherman and Farmer 30 March 1888*)

*12 Lee, John F. (*Fisherman and Farmer 3 February 1888*)

*13 Miller, Silas (*Fisherman and Farmer 4 October 1889*)

*14 Creecy, Alfred (*Fisherman and Farmer 16 November 1888; Fisherman and Farmer 8 June 1894*)

*15 Reed, Rial (*Fisherman and Farmer 30 March 1888*)

*16 Holley, Willis (*Fisherman and Farmer 14 October 1887*)

*17 Jones, Vandon (*Fisherman and Farmer 1 March, 1889*)

*18 Sawyer, James (*Fisherman and Farmer 16 February 1894; 2 March 1894*)

*19 Knight, Simond P. (*Fisherman and Farmer 16 December 1892*)

*20 Tillery, Louis (*Fisherman and Farmer 11 November 1892*)

Chapter 1

1870

"Making a Way Out of No Way"

The 1870 census was the first census after the Civil War, and the abolition of slavery, that all African-Americans who had lived as slaves were counted, with full names and surnames. Heads of household, their spouses and children, and other family and friends living with them, were delineated as units. Here is where we find our ancestors as people, trying to make life work, through the 1865-1877 period known as Reconstruction.

Edenton's records regarding this time period are minimal, in part due to the minor involvement the town and county in general had in the war. Some Union sympathizers and groups known as "Buffaloes" made havoc in the rural areas, but rarely came into town. In February of 1862, the Federal fleet arrived at Edenton. Residents thought they were about to be bombarded. There were no problems, however. The sailors were friendly. They came ashore for provisions, and paid for them. There was little to no physical damage, because it was of little strategic consequence. Edenton was unfortified during the war, and became neutral ground for both Confederates and Federals.

The most devastating effect the Civil War had upon Chowan County was in the area of its economics. Although there were no serious battles and lootings, its traditional wealth in slaves and land was gone, leading to a depression. Many planters, fishery owners and merchants lost their wealth. Great plantation estates were sold off in small tracts of land, and turned into small farms.

Newly freed blacks became farmers of their own lands; acquired by the subdivision of plantations, government sales of abandoned and confiscated lands, and estate sales. In 1862, some plantations of Confederate leaders were subdivided by Union generals. Some former slaves obtained land by it being given to them by former owners, if those owners had feelings of benevolence towards them. Some masters sold property to their former slaves for small fees, and some specified that after their deaths, land should be sold to their slaves.

By 1870, nearly 4,000 black men who were heads of household owned real estate, but only a few are mentioned in land deeds that were registered in the late 1860s. This might make it difficult for you to find your ancestors in the deeds office. I have yet to find out exactly HOW my great-great-great grandfather came to live on his land, and in what part of Edenton he lived, but by 1870, his son lived on King Street with his wife and children.

Farmers and Laborers

Here then, listed by census page, are the names of heads of household in 1870, who were farmers and laborers. The term "laborers" could mean any kind of work. Women heads of household were often listed as "domestics". Their work consisted of cooking, cleaning, and child care of the families in which they were employed.

Census Page

1: Collins, Isaac; **Johnson**, Aaron; **Johnson**, Allen; **Johnson**, David (or Daniel); **Johnson**, Mack; **Ruci** (?), James; **Skinner**, Arnato (or Arnold); **Smith**, Cambridge.

2: Brownrigg, Fred; **Collins**, Samuel; **Foxwell**, Alfred; **Gregory**, Harry; **Johnson**, John; **White**, Virgil; **Williams**, Charles.

3: Bond, Augustus; **Bond**, Henry; **Drew**, William; **Hudgins**, George; **Hurdle**, Charles; **Nixon**, Squire.

4: Goodwin, Stephen; **Jackson**, John; **Jones**, America; **Satterfield**, Tredwell; **Treadwell**, Frank.

5: Benbury, Shadrack; **Bond**, Thomas; **Harris**, Washington; **Right**, Stephen; **Rumbolt**, John; **Wynn**, Alexander.

3

6: Benton, Biddy; **Bond**, Joe; **Bond**, Rose; **Coffield**, Phillis; **Haughton**, Emanuel; **Johnson**, D.; **Launner**, Thomas; **Warren**, Primus; **Winn**, Fred; **Wright**, Sarah.

7: Bond, Harry; **Kane**, Peter; **Leary**, Spencer; **Warner**, Charity; **Wilder**, Charles; **Wilder**, Thomas.

8: Bond, John; **Bond**, Joseph; **Harris**, Dennis; **Hunter**, Miley; **Hunter**, Virgil; **Satterfield**, Isaac; **White**, Lewis, **Wiggins**, L.

9: Blount, Anthony; **Bond**, David; **Bond**, Gaston; **Bonner** (?), John; **Hoskins**, Frances; **Leary**, Washington; **Rhodes**, Daniel; **Valentine**, Alexander.

10: Morris, David; **Warren**, Austin; **Warren**, Hardy.

11: Brown, Marko; **Creecy**, Jerry; **Johnson**, Alfred; **Skinner**, Henry; **Spencer**, John.

12: Leary, Jerry; **Mebane**, Frank; **Price**, James; **Ward**, Daniel (white, married to Easther, black; children mulatto); **Warren**, Margaret; **Whidbee**, Edward; **Whidbee**, Simeon.

13: Faton (?), John; **Jones**, William; **Welch**, Robert, **Wilder**, Mike.

14: Bond, Major; **Bunch**, Franke; **Newbern**, Miles; **Skinner**, Daniel; **Wilkins**, John.

15: All residents on this page are white.

16: Wright, Gregory.

17: Bullock, Major; **Skinner**, Simon.

18: Blount, George; **Brown**, Easter; **Paxton**, Robert; **Ryan**, Thadius; **Skinner**, John.

19: Badham, Albert; **Hoskins**, Stephen; **Jordan**, Wesley; **Lyles**, Warren; **Skinner**, Andrew; **Skinner**, James; **Skinner**, Nelly; **Williams**, George.

20: Clark, James; **Creighton**, Albert; **Deal**, Priscilla; **Houghton**, Richard; **Lowther**, Charles; **Lowther**, Isaac.

21: Blount, Anthony; **Blount**, James; **Creecy**, John; **Gilliam**, Peterson; **Gilliam**, Thompson; **McCluci**(?); James.

22: Parker, Moses; **Paxton**, Abram; **Skinner**, Peter; **Snowden**, Isaac; **Waff**, George.

23: Simpson, Richard; **Waff**, Frank; **Walters**, Mary.

24: Jeff, Armstrong; **Bricks**, Luke; **Davis**, William; **Perkins**, Atlas; **Skinner**, Perry; **Standing**; George; **Sutton**, Ransom.

25: Benbury, Edward; **Harrell**, Cassandra; **Hoskins**, Moses.

26: Benbury, Isaac; **Carter**, George; **Moore**, Louisa; **Parrish**, Sandy; **Stallings**, Ostin; **Stallings**, Washington; **Stallings**, William.

27: Eason, John; **Fleetwood**, Fn?agh(?); **Jordan**, Henry; **Long**, John; **Nixon**, James.

28: Lawrence, Thomas; **Mitchell**, Catherine; **Skinner**, Caroline; **Trotman**, Ham(?)

29: Hagins, John; **Harris**, Andy; **Harris**, Judy; **Petigrew**, Anthony.

30: Brown, William; **Bullock**, Moses; **Burke**, Major; **Cabarrus**, Pulliam; **Hinton**, Thomas; **Thatch**, Cherry.

31: Cabarrus, Noah; **Collins**, Joseph; **Haughton**, Solomon; **Haughton**, Thomas; **Jones**, Martha; **Little**, Hamilton; **Page**, Lonan; **Pot(?)**, Patience; **Sawyer**, John; **Wills**, John.

32: Armstead, David; **Blount**, Thancy; **Bond**, Willis, **Cabarrus**, Truman; **Collins**, Miles; **Dickerson**, Andrew; **Gilbert**, Rose; **Houghton**, Alexander; **Wills**, Thomas.

33: Drew, Jacob; **Moon**, Margaret; **Robins**, Comfort, **Skinner**, James; **Wrighton**, Miles.

34: Bond, George; **Cook**, Frank; **Drew**, Taylor; **Lamb**, John; **Reddick**, Langston; **Saunders**, Mike; **Simpson**, Nelson.

35: Blanchard, John; **Blount**, Mills; **Gregory**, Wilson; **Perkins**, Major; **Swan**, Thomas.

36: Cambrell, Thomas; **Hoskins**, Thomas; **Jerkins**, Richard; **Jordan**, Samuel; **Lutten**, Jordan; **Paxton**, Nat; **Roberts**, Nelly; **Skinner**, Nelson.

37: Johnson, Anthony; **M(?)**, Joseph; **Overton**, Charlotte; **Paxton**, Charles; **Sawyer**, Dinah; **Shannonhouse**, Alfonso; **Smith**, Harrison; **Waff**, Martha; **Wilson**, Cornelius.

38: Benton, Reuben; **Bizzell**, Joseph; **Bond**, Anthony; **Dail**, Isaac; **Gatling**, Silvey; **Johnson**, Wills; **Overton**, Kate; **Paxton**, John; **Roberts**, Glasgow; **Sutton**, Anderson.

39: Beasley, Mary; **Clarke**, Fanny; **Creecy**, Jacob; ***1-Gilliam**, Atlas; **Johnson**, Primus; **Nixon**, Charity; **Nixon**, Margaret; **Paxton**, Abram.

Clipped from Fisherman and Farmer, 18 Apr 1890, Fri, First Edition, Page 5

A Good Woman Dead.

Amie Gilliam, one of the best old colored women of our town, is dead. She died Saturday morning and was buried Sunday evening. Her funeral procession was one of the largest we ever saw in Edenton and was composed of both races. She was a devoted Christian and a member of the A. M. E. Zion Church. In her death our colored people have felt a great loss, and we extend our deepest sympathy to the bereaved.

40: **Johnson,** Lunon; **Paxton,** David.

41: Paxton, James; **Whitley,** Nancy.

42: Blount, Henry; **Cox**, Harry; **Davis**, Washington; **Hoskins**, John; **Johnson**, Silvy; **Nixon**, Della; **Paxton**, Joseph; **Perkins**, Grace; **Sawyer**, Zel.

43: Benbury, Shadrack; **Felton**, Richard; **Perkins**, Isaac; **Skinner**, John; **Skinner**, Moses; **Trip**, Robert.

44: Benbury, Abram; **Benbury**, Lawrence; **Blair**, Henderson; **Blount**, Eliza; **Steward**, Isiah; **Wynn**, Richard.

45: Ryan, Sally; **Whidbee**, Albert.

46: Baoran (?), Lucy; **Beasley**, Annis; **Beasley**, Fillis; **Felton**, Jonah; **Sutton**, Jonas; **Vaughn**, Jonas.

47: Bunch, Samuel; **Creecy**, Frank; **Jordan**, Joseph; **Thach**, Joshua.

48: Hall, Jacob; **Hall**, Penelope; **Page**, Hartkis; **Thompson**, Page; **Standing**, Mack; **Wilder**, Boston.

49: Blount, Allen; **Blount**, Henry; **Copeland**, Solomon; **Gussom**, Christiana; **Leary**, Thompson; **Owens**, Isaac; **Wilson**, Robert.

50: Blair, Penelope; **Blount**, Alley; **Nixon**, Arthur; **Small**, Abigail.

51: Jones, William; **Waff**, Thomas.

52: Runnels, Hamilton.

53: Columbus, Jordan; **Furman**, Arthur; **Picke**, MaryJane; **Ria**, James; **Small**, Thomas; **Taylor**, Joseph; **White**, Jerry.

54: Asbell, Artist; **Bosley**, John; **Brady**, Stephen; **Henry**, Judy; **Hoskins**, Charles, **Milton**, Ely; **Norcum**, Edward; **Small**, Mills.

55: Felton, Chloe; **Skinner**, Augustus; **Skinner**, Fred; **Wrighton**, Mack.

56: Davis, Harvey; **Freeman**, William; **Sells**, Thomas.

57: Benbury, Caine; **Hinton**, Calvin; **Page**, Nathan; **Simpson**, Arter.

58: Halsey, Isaac; **Hathaway**, Anthony.

59: Granbury, Harrison (Harmon); **Hinton**, David; **Nixon**, Thomas; **Roberts**, Armstead; **Roberts**, Haywood; **Skinner**, Harry.

60: Belch, Mills; **Farand**, Mary; **Harnet**, Simon; **Johnson**, Marcella; **Leary**, Robert; **Norcum**, Julia; **Sharp**, Abram; **Taylor**, Isaac; **Wright**, Harry (Harvey).

61: Gilliam, Henry; **Haughton**, Richard; **Leary** Jr., Ephram A.; **Nixon**, Moses; **Wright**, Harry.

62: Benbury, Augustus; **Benbury**, Charles; **Benbury**, Leon; **Benbury**, Wilson; **Goodwin**, Miles; **Ransom**, George; **Robinson**, Joseph.

63: Blount, Charles; **Blount**, Virgil; **Blount**, William; **Leary**, Robert; **Wills**, Jacob.

64: Birnett, Charity; **Blount**, Maxwell; **Fry**, Robert; **Gregory**, Charles; **Leary**, Thomas; **Orange**, John; **Osten**, Gregory; **Picier (?)**, Mingo; **Wilson**, Stephen.

9

65: **Banks**, Andrew; **Gatling**, Joseph; **Hathaway**, Nelson, **Hathaway**, Taylor; **Haughton**, Jeffry; **Manning**, C.M.; **Scott**, John; **Skinner**, Richard; **Skinner**, Richard (two of them).

66: **Gregory**, Fanny; **Gregory**, Henry; **Harvey**, Richard; **Hathaway**, Joseph; **Skinner**, Charles; **Skinner**, Lydia; **Wells**, James.

67: **Blair**, William; **Blount**, Wilson; **Lowther**, Sipeo; **Lowther**, Wilson; **Skinner**, Allen; **Washington**, Halsey.

68: **Gregory**, Joseph; **Lil__?**, Philip; **Mul__?**, Henry.

69: **Harvey**, George; **Johnson**, Da__?; **Moon**, Andrew.

70: **Bruce**, Harry; **Faribault**, Henderson.

71: **Clarke**, John; **Dempsey**, William; **Jones**, Hetty; **Johnson**, Lewis; **Louther**, Clarissa; **Riddick**, Jennett; **Tucker**, Henry.

72: **Akerson**, William; **Charleton**, George; **Jones**, Hetty; **Leary**, William; **Nichols**, Henry; **Nixon**, Easter (Eartha); **Williams**, Hester.

73: **Haughton**, Patsmer/Palsmer/Palmer; **Johnson**, Stephen; **Watkins**, Francis.

74: **Blair**, Clarissa; **Nixon**, William; **Picard**, Horace; **Roberts**, Hester; **Wood**, Joesph.

75: **Benbury**, Chison; **Benbury**, Craven; **Blanchard**, Edward; **Gaskins**, Marinda; **Haughton**, Flora; **Haughton**, James; **Page**, Eliza; **Paxton**, Samuel; **Tredwell**, Nelly; **Whidbee**, James.

76: Banks, Washington; **Best**, Noah; **Gibbs**, Anderson; **Hill**, Abram; **Miller**, Silas; **Rumbo**, Abram; **Thomas**, Daniel.

77: Daves Harvey; **Jackson**, Mary; **James**, Betty; **Jordan**, Penelope.

78: Alexander, Thomas; **Bennett**, Allen; **Bond**, Charles; **Drew**, Rebecca; **Faribauls**, Matilda; **Johnson**, Gilly; **Mardis**, David; **Mealeson**, Amy; **Nixon**, John; **Skinner**, William; **White**, H__?; **Wilder**, Annie.

79: Blount, Whilmel; **Hudgins**, William; **Jordon**, Theodon; **Morgan**, Aaron.

80: Wrighton, Peter.

81: Gilbert, Harriet (domestic in home of Oliver Gilbert); **Jones**, Pattie(?) (domestic in home of John Jones); **Wood**, Clara (domestic in home of William Wood).

82: Benbury, Samuel; **Blount**, Mills; **Faribault**, Chloe; **Outlaw**, Lusa; **Regan**, Pattie; **Rumbo**, Mathias.

83: Blount, Alfred; **Cheshire**, Thomas; **Jones**, Harriet; **Jones**, Joseph; **Jones**, Richard; **Page**, Benjamin; **Paxton**, John.

84: Bond, Peter; **Carpenter**, Simon; **Cooper**, Paul; **Elliott**, Anderson; **Nixon**, Edward; **Ramsey**, Ann; **Skinner**, Richard.

85: Badham, Hester.

86: Skipped because of special labor category, listed separately.

87: Beasely, Larry; **Beasely**, Margaret; **Farmer**, L__nia; **Lowther**, Anthony; **Simons**, Betty; **Skinner**, Jacob; **Wynn**, Joseph.

88: Blount, Malvina; **Lowther**, William.

89: Skipped because of special labor category, listed separately.

90: Jones, Mary; **Norcum**, Harry; **Simpson**, Samuel; **Whidbee**, John.

91: Cox, Isaac; **Hassell**, Anderson; **Satterfield**, Pherebe; **Sawyer**, Sarah; **Skinner**, Edy; **Steward**, Jane; **Wynn**, David.

92: *2-Mayho, Edward; **McDonald**, Betty.

Clipped from **Fisherman and Farmer**, **13 Apr 1888, Fri**, **First Edition**

DROPPED DEAD.

On Tuesday morning, Edward Mayo, a highly respected colored man, while at Branning & Bro's. mill loading his cart with slab wood, died very sudden. It seems that his colt, which he had trained and loved as a child, had taken fright and began to run; the old man immediately ran after him. The horse went for some distance and, overturning the cart, fell to the ground, sticking into his leg an iron hook attached to the cart shaft. In a moment several arrived to the spot and began to loose the horse. Mayo arrived just as the hook was drawn from the horse's leg and seeing it, exclaimed,

"LORD, MY COLT IS RUINED !"

falling instantly dead. The coronor had him sent home and Dr. Hoskins summoned. The doctor examined him but soon announced that death had done its work. Mayo was a good citizen and had lived in Edenton a number of years. He was buried yesterday.

Barbers

Many free blacks found work as barbers.

Blacks became barbers because many white men did not want to take on occupations that seemed like servitude. Barbering gave other African Americans opportunities, including young men who became apprentices to established barbers. More information can be found in the book, *Knights of the Razor: Black Barbers in Slavery and Freedom,* by Douglas Walter Bristol, Jr.

In the 1870 census, there was only one African American person in Edenton who was a barber. His name was **Sylvester Dunston**. He was able to read and write. An article in the February 22, 1917 edition of The New York Age had news about its colored citizens from Raleigh, NC. On page 5, it states *"Sylvester Dunston, an aged citizen, died at his home last Monday night and was buried from St. Paul's A.M.E. church last Thursday. Reverend A.D. Avery officiated."* It is not clear if it is the same Sylvester Dunston. Further research is warranted.

Barkeeper

One African American was listed as a barkeeper, that being **James Lee**. James was listed in the household of David Lee, a gunsmith and jeweler. He was probably David's brother, as there was also in the household a 64-year-old woman by the name of Sidney. She may have been their mother. It is not known where James worked as a barkeeper. It may possibly have been at the Woodard Hotel.

Blacksmith

The process of making tools and sculptures from iron is both a skill and a craft that many of our ancestors brought from Africa. They developed and passed down this skill, or they were taught the skill from others here in America. In the south, slaves were trained in iron-making and the heavy and hot work of handling iron was given to slave labor. Slaves were expected to make everything that was created from iron-everything from horseshoes to carriage and wagon frames, to kitchen utensils and iron gates. After Emancipation, this was an occupation in demand and many men continued in this trade. Blacksmiths held a position of extreme importance in the community; so much of people's daily lives depended on their work.

Horses need shoes, wagon wheels needed rims, and plows, rails and tools may have needed repair. The status of the blacksmith or ironworker in the community was high. In Edenton, an 1870 listing of products and industry showed a Hamilton Johnson as owning his own blacksmith shop. In addition to Johnson, there were six other men whose occupation was blacksmith in the 1870 census: **Provey Cox** (the author's g-g-g grandfather); **Henry James, Mus__? McDonald, John Sawyer, George Skinner,** and **John Skinner.**

Brick Masons

Brick makers were an important part of the labor force in the south, as shown through the large numbers of brick structures throughout the region. The process involved digging clay from the ground, building molds and frames to shape the clay, drying the bricks in the air, then burning them for weeks in the kiln.

The kiln itself was made of stacked bricks so that when they were sufficiently dried by slow fire, the entire kiln was dismantled, and the bricks used in building.

The skill of laying bricks for building purposes was also needed. Constructing houses, chimneys, and churches were all part of the brick mason's abilities. Four men were found in the 1870 census whose occupation was that of brick mason: **Job Charleston, John King, Sampson Riddick,** and **Larkin Smith**.

Carpenter

They made coffins, cabinets, chairs, and interior decorations, and their stories are told, and found in the material artifacts in many stages of our country's development. From slaves to freemen, African-American artisans were extremely important. Slaves were purchased with the slaveholders' understanding that the people were able to learn handicrafts and make a specific contribution to the success of the farm, shop, or plantation. They realized the importance and impact of this, so the owner would identify their brightest, most industrious and, perhaps, most creative slaves. The owners would see to it that they learned, usually as an apprentice, one of the essential trades, including blacksmithing, masonry, and carpentry. The genius and skill of those slaves is evident today in old southern mansions, churches and many other public buildings, as well as in house museums and private collections. The following men were listed in the 1870 census as house carpenters. Many of them are mentioned in Thomas Butchko's extensive work, *Edenton: An Architectural Portrait*. Carpenters who lived in other townships can be found in his book, in Appendix H.

Badham, Hannibal; **Badham,** Miles (prominent builders, mentioned in Butchko's book); **Banks,** Washington; **Beasly,** Henry; **Benbridge,** Noah; **Benbury,** John; **Blair,** Jordan; **Carter,** George; **Costen,** Joseph; **Eden,** Exum; **Heath,** William; **Johnson,** Henry; **Jones,** Peter; **Jordan,** Elijah; **King,** Peter; **Lowther,**

Henry; **Lowther,** William; **McDonald,** Isaac; **Murphy,** Kellis (mentioned in Butchko's book); **Page,** John; and **Price,** Joseph.

Edenton's survival at this time depended on bounty from the sea-through seine fishing, brought to shore at the wooden wharves and piers. Boats were built of wood, and there was also a need for carpenters to make repairs, keep the boats waterproof and generally work on them in whatever way was necessary. Two men were listed as ship carpenters: **Charles Lowther** and **Davy Perkins.**

Clergy

There is no question as to the importance of the Black church throughout history. From before Emancipation to this present day, the church has served to help create and nurture new citizens and leaders of slaves and former slaves; and develop communities through education, and relief of the poor. It was, and is the platform for creating politicians and everyday citizens who are empowered to demand social action against injustices. Edenton's documentation of the organization of black churches there can be found in the edition of *Images of America: Edenton and Chowan County* by Louis Van Camp; and Thomas Butchko's book. The histories of Kadesh A.M.E. Zion Church (organized in 1866), Pleasant Grove A.M.E. Zion Church (organized in 1866), Providence Baptist Church (organized in 1868), St. John the Evangelist Episcopal (organized in 1881), and Gale Street Baptist Church (organized in 1895) are noted in those books.

Only one person was listed as "clergy" in the 1870 census. It is not clear if he was an itinerant preacher, or in charge of any of the early churches there. His name was **John Williams.** Further research is warranted.

Constable

The status of black policemen in southern cities and towns was controversial. They did not have authority and responsibility to arrest their white neighbors, but to only police their communities and stay in their place. No newspapers for 1870 Edenton seem to exist. Yet, **Peter Jones** was identified as the town constable in the 1870 census. He was probably responsible for policing the "colored" section of the community, but since no newspapers for 1870 Edenton seem to exist, it is not known how he came to have this employment.

Cook in Hotel

Sometime before 1874, there was a hotel in Edenton owned by Richard Woodard. The Woodard Hotel, according to Butchko, "was one of the town's largest and most modern hotels" (p.106). Richard Woodard was listed in the 1870 census on page 88 as a "hotel keeper". Listed in his household, with the same surname as his, was **Jennie Woodard**, a black woman, age 50. She served as a cook in his hotel. Having the same surname implies that she may have been among his slaves, and after Emancipation, she stayed on with Woodard and his family.

Cooper

A cooper is a person whose work is making or repairing barrels and casks. A person who was able to do this did an important job, as many things were stored and shipped in barrels. Everything from food to wine, to turpentine was stored in barrels. The making of barrels was usually taught to slaves, by the barrel maker on the plantation where they lived. **Walker Henry** was listed as a cooper in the 1870 census.

Merchant

There are a few studies on the rise of African American merchants and business owners in the post-war south. The most common types of black businesses were grocery, provision, confectionary, and general merchandise dealers. In Edenton, there were six credit-rated black firms, according to the R.G. Dunn & Co. Credit Ledgers 1865-79. Four men listed as merchants, were found in the 1870 census: **Charles Blair, David Blount, Frank Cheshire,** and **David Lee**. Looking forward, the 1880 census gave the businesses for two of them. David Lee was a jeweler and gunsmith, and a highly respected man in both the black and white communities. It is not known how he was able to develop a business in those two very specialized areas, because understandably, very few white southerners would want a Negro having access to guns. A study about black business owners found that more than half of them were mulattos. This may have been because they were free in 1860, which may have given them an "edge" over the recently freed people, as they were able to continue the antebellum business they had. Lee, Cheshire and Blair were mulattos. This David Lee was born in Virginia in about 1832. He may have been an apprentice to a gunsmith in Virginia, before he came to Edenton. In May of 1899, he wrote a commentary about building housing for residents, in the *Fisherman and Farmer*. In August of 1890, he wrote of his plan for moving his jewelry and gunsmith shop to a lot on East Queen Street. In 1880, David Blount was listed as a mattress maker. Neither Frank Cheshire nor Charles Blair was found in 1880, so there is no listing as to what their businesses were. By 1880, Frank's wife Lucy was head of household, so Frank may have died. His youngest child was born in 1872.

Painter

There was one person named as a painter in the 1870 census. His name was **Dorsey Steward/Stewart**. His father, **Isam Stewart** was also a painter, and was free in 1860. Apparently these two had substantial responsibility for painting the Chowan County Courthouse, for they are known to have painted the interior of the building in 1836, 1850, 1869, and 1904.

Shoemaker

There was only one person found in the town of Edenton whose occupation was a shoemaker. His name was **Reuben Wright.**

Waterman

Edenton's livelihood and economic strength was based on the fishing business at its wharves. Fishing was done with a seine, a type of net that hangs vertically in the water. Its bottom edge is held down by weights, and its top edge is buoyed by floats. When its ends are pulled closed, it catches the fish. Shad and herring were the product.

In addition to fishing, Edenton's waterways during the antebellum period were part of the Underground Railroad. Harriet Jacobs escaped from Edenton with help from the African American community, and black seamen.

The occupation of waterman could mean any job from fishing, to possibly working as a steward or cook. Other jobs men held were painting, caulking and repairing ships or boats. The following men were listed as watermen: **Jerry Bennett, Joseph Blount Alfred Creecy, Henry Dempsey, John Draper; Rial Reed, Mebane Ruffin,** and **Damon Spellman.**

Chapter 2

1880

"Revive Us Again"

The 1880s saw a dramatic increase in the types of labor in which black residents were engaged. As the town grew, so did the diversity of occupations and services that were not only made available to Edenton's residents, but also and more importantly, invented, nurtured and developed by our ancestors. They took the initiative and broke the color line by offering needed services-- actively pursuing that which would push Edenton into the 19th century. The county as a whole was still farm-based. Even those who had other trades or professions still relied on farming as a major source of income. The fascinating part now, is that the actions and lives of some of these people merit being included in various articles of the "Colored News" section of the *Fisherman and Farmer*. Now we can see them as whole people, with individual and family lives and personalities, and we can get a glimpse of how they lived through published documentation. As before, any person found to have an article mention will have an asterisk by his or her name. The article immediately follows.

Listings will be similar to the 1870 census. Those who stated that they were farmers, domestics/housekeepers, and laborers will be grouped by census page. Those who had more specific occupations will be listed under the name of the occupation, and historical content will be added for some of them. Descriptions of new occupations will be included in this chapter.

There is a note written by the census taker at the end of the 1880 census that states: "One great reason for the small increase in the population of this town is that by an act of the Legislature of this state was the town charter of said town so amended that a large part of Northerdly side of said town was excluded from the corporation limits, and thereby deprives said town of one hundred and eighty two inhabitants all of which are mulattoes and blacks."

That means the one hundred and eighty two individuals are missing from the Edenton Town census, many of whom may have been in the 1870 census. How, or if they were counted at all, or included in some other part of Edenton is unclear. Readers are encouraged to look through the four pages of the "Town Commons" section of the county, for those individuals and others, since this book focuses on Edenton Town.

Laborers and Farmers

Following is the listing of heads of household of the town, who stated their occupation as farmer, laborer, or domestic.

Census Page

1. **Ryan**, Pattie; **Wilson**, Smith.

2. **King**, Henry; **Little**, Jordan; **Pruden**, Thomas; **Sawyer**, Zall; **Underhill**, Nelson; **Woodley**, Llewellyn.

3. **Brinkley**, James; **Haughton**, Mary; **Johnston**, Anthony; **Johnston**, Wells; **Kellam**, Jacob; **Lowther**, Graham; **Paxton**, Charles; **Pierce**, Sherman; **Whitley**, Nancy.

4. **Beasley**, Tony; **Eason**, Henry; **Gregory**, Austin; **Gregory**, John; **Grice**, Anthony; **Hill**, Caroline; **Johnston**, Caroline; **Johnston**, Giah; **Page**, Laura.

5. **Cheshire**, Lucy; **Collins**, Alice; **Faribault**, Cloe; **Jones**, Mary; **Nixon**, Charity; **Page**, Jane; **Skinner**, Jane; ***3- Sutton**, Edward; **Williams**, Philip.

6. **Best**, Noah; **Cheshire**, Thomas; **Johnston**, London; **Smith**, George; **Wilder**, Boston.

7. **Harrell**, Anderson; **Faribault**, Prince A.; **Murdough**, David.

8. **Bond**, Sarah; **Coleman**, Jacob; **Felton**, Pleasant; **Gilliam**, Sallie; **Gregory**, Joseph.

9. **Haughton**, Melvina; **Picott**, Annie; **Skinner**, Treecy/Tracy.

10. **Banks**, Jennetta; **Haughton**, Jeffrey; **Haughton**, Melvina; **Muse**, Nathaniel; **Smith**, David; **White**, Harriet.

11. **Bizzell**, Venus; **Charlton**, Annie; ***4-McGee**, William; **Paxton**, Charity; ***5-Skinner**, Jacob.

12. **Nixon**, Mary; **Roberts**, Glasgow.

13. **Daves**, Armstead; **Rumbough**, Abram; **Thomas**, Martha; **Wilkins**, Ann.

14. **Goodwin**, Elijah; **Gregory**, Silvia; **Johnston**, Hester; **Outlaw**, Edy; **Sutton**, Susan; **Whedbee**, Jenny.

15. **Hyman**, Matilda; **Norcon (Norcum)**, Carolina; **Paxton**, Fannie.

16. **Eppes**, Ransom; **Nixon**, Isaac; **Wilder**, Walter.

17. Beasley, Jerry; **Griffin**, Mozella; **Mayo**, Edward; **Whedbee**, Louisia.

Clipped from Fisherman and Farmer, 20 Jul 1888, Fri, First Edition, Page 4

JAILED AND DRIVEN FROM HOME.

A COLORED NORTH CAROLINA RE-PUBLICAN TELLS OF DEMO-CRATIC PERSECUTION.

Under the above head the following article appeared in the "Philadelphia Press," as stated by Edward H. Sutton—a dirty negro who left Edenton some months since and who is now in Philadelphia. Read the article:

"Edward H. Sutton, colored, ex-member of the North Carolina Legislature, has arrived in town and will tell some remarkable stories of the treatment of his race in North Carolina during the coming campaign.

28

(cont'd.)

He says in regard to the writing of his book : 'I did it, not to show that I hold any malice against those who persecuted me for my Republicanism. I cherish nothing but the warmest feeling for them. Their persecution certainly made me a smarter man than if I had been out of jail. I was twice in jail before I was elected to the Legislature. and, strange to say, I have yet for the first time to hurt any man in Chowan county. The public know too much of the suffering of the Southern negro, but I can tell them a thing a two that they do not know, and I am glad that I am in a State where I can express my thoughts and knowledge without being sent to prison.'

(cont'd.)

While in prison Mr. Sutton received a letter of sympathy from Gen. John A. Logan. Mr. Sutton will place himself in the hands of the Campaign Committee and do anything in his power for the ticket. He is compelled to stay away from his home and family in North Carolina owing to the hatred of the white politicians against him. Since he has been away from Chowan two of his children have died."

Clipped from <u>Fisherman and Farmer</u>, <u>12 Oct 1888, Fri</u>, <u>First Edition</u>

properly registered.

One Hundred Thousand Dollars! Whoo-pee? It would be wiser if he would join the Prohibitionists. Perhaps he would then have a little left after the 6th of November.

Sheriff J. C. Warren escorted this week Lewis Creech and Will McGee, (colored) to the State's boarding house where they will remain for one and three years respectively.

Mr. A. French, representing the American Net & Twine Co., of New York, gave us a pleasant visit this week. Woodard Bros. will take orders for the company in Mr. French's absence.

ICE CREAM AND TAFFY
The BEST Made

Can be found every day at Market Stall No. 4.

Orders for suppers &c will be filled on short notice at low prices.
A trial is all I want.

The Old Reliable,

Jacob Skinner.

18. Brown, Delia; **Nixon**, William.

19. Badham, Prince A.; **Blair**, Clarissa; **Churden**, Theodore; **Collins**, Matilda; **Gorham**, Annie; **Johnston**, Sarah; **Skinner**, Peter; **Skinner**, Violet; **Williams**, George.

20. Collins, Hessie; **Drew**, Rebecca (both legs off); **Louther**, Clarisa; **Paxton**, Jane; **Whedbee**, Hester.

21. Davis, Washington; **Latham**, Millicent; **Lee**, Marcia; **Whedbee**, James.

22. Badham, Hester; **Bembury**, Celia; **Blair**, Mary; **Blount**, Eliza; **Gordon**, Sophelia; **Lowther**, William; **Mixon**, Hardy; **Rumbough**, Mathias; **Turner**, Tamer.

23. Cox, Isaac; **Harvey**, Osborne; **Jordan**, Ellen; **Skinner**, Edy.

24. Perry, Catherine; **Simpson**, Susan.

25. Benbury, Samuel; **Bunch**, Anthony; **Roberts**, Nelly; **Wilder**, William.

26. All white and prisoners at county jail.

27. Goodwin, Julia; **Harrell**, Annie; **Johnston**, Rufus.

28. Cheshire, Hester; **Paxton**, Jenny.

29. Bond, Charles

30. Turner, Florence

Baker

James Jones, baker, likely made many things we enjoy today: bread, rolls, biscuits, pies and cakes, even pretzels. By 1880, he may have had a kitchen stove with an oven, heated with wood or charcoal, or he may have still baked in a small oven built off to the side of a brick fireplace. A baker spent many long hours at work, keeping the fire stoked all night, up early to knead the dough, watching for just the right amount of golden crust when the bread was done. Jones's wife, Martha, is shown in the census as "assists in baking," which may indicate they had a thriving business.

Barbers: *6-Leary, Sweety; **Williams**, Octavious.

Clipped from <u>Fisherman and Farmer</u>, <u>16 Nov 1888, Fri</u>, <u>First Edition</u>, <u>Page 5</u>

Swety Leary's barber shop has again received new additions and been brightened by new touches of the painter's brush. Swety is a genius. Had he received an early training in the art of painting he would have been as good with pencil and brush as he now is with razor and scissors.

Basket Maker

Weaving, braiding and coiling natural fibers into baskets is a craft with its roots in Africa. Perhaps it was a skill handed down through generations of **Henry Iredell**'s family. Iredell had a "deformed right leg from birth," so he was fortunate to find an occupation that did not rely on physical strength, but on dexterity and skill. Baskets were created in a variety of shapes and sizes, and were the commonplace way of carrying goods on one's arm, on one's head, or in wagons. Basket makers also wove strainers and sifters, traps, hats, chair bottoms, belts, window shades and sleeping mats. White oak, palmetto leaves, pine needles and corn husks were among the materials used in basket making.

Blacksmiths: Blount, Joseph B.; *7- **James**, Henry; **Little**, Frances; **McDonald**, Mustipher; **Miles**, Tatem; **Skinner**, John L.

Boots/Shoes: Gatling, Joseph; *8-**Tillery**, Lewis (Louis).

Brickmen: Charlton, Edward; **Charlton**, Job; **Luten**, Anderson; **Norcom**, John; **Smith**, Larken

Clipped from <u>Fisherman and Farmer</u>, <u>07 Oct 1887, Fri</u>, <u>First Edition</u>, <u>Page 1</u>

Henry James (colored,) not appreciating the danger, stored fodder in a portion of his blacksmith shop which, on Tuesday, caught fire from a spark emitted by the forge, consuming the building and somewhat damaging two other houses adjacent thereto.

Clipped from <u>Fisherman and Farmer</u>, <u>06 Jan 1888, Fri</u>, <u>First Edition</u>, <u>Page 2</u>

Clipped from <u>Fisherman and Farmer</u>, <u>22 Apr 1892, Fri</u>, <u>First Edition</u>, <u>Page 8</u>

Mr Louis Tillery has returned home again, and hereafter can be found at his same old stand on Main street at all hours. Call and see him.

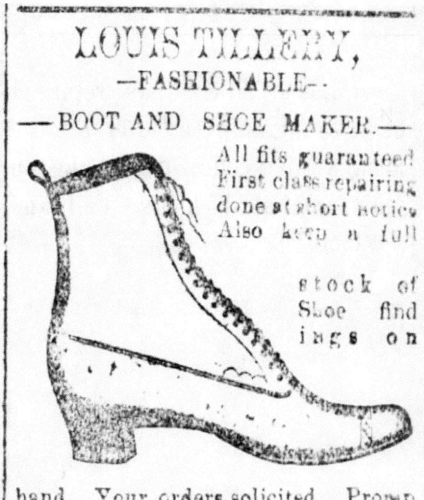

LOUIS TILLERY,
—FASHIONABLE—

——BOOT AND SHOE MAKER.——

All fits guaranteed
First class repairing
done at short notice
Also keep a full

stock of
Shoe find
ings on

hand. Your orders solicited. Promp
Attention. Call and see me. Main St
Edenton, N. C.

Butcher

When **Moses Skinner** was a butcher in Edenton, pork was the staple meat. Hogs were more manageable than cows. They gave birth to large litters, and they were easier to feed. Pork could be smoked, dried and salted, the only means of preserving meat in an era before refrigeration. It is not known where Skinner did the butchering, or whether he sold cuts of meat. He may have gone to farms and butchered the meat on site for a fee, or people may have brought him hogs, deer, turkeys and other game to be butchered.

Butler

The title of butler, given to the senior man servant in a household, was not in common usage in rural North Carolina. This man was entrusted with the keys to the wine cellars, the pantry and other valuables, and had substantial responsibilities. **Stant** (or **Staut**) **Skinner** was identified as a butler at age 40, but there is no information as to who employed him. One of the first books written by an African American was "The House Servants Directory," a handbook for butlers and waiters, published in 1827. The author, Robert Roberts, worked for several prominent families in Massachusetts.

Carpenter

Badham, Hannibal; *9-**Beasley,** Henry; **Benbury,** Noah; **Benbury,** Thomas; **Blair,** Jordan; **Blanchard,** Edward; **Blount,** Edward; **Carter,** George; **Charlton,** Job; **Collen,** Duvick(?); **Edes,** Exum; **Hathaway,** Elijah; **Heath,** William; **Hurdle,** Charles; **Iredell,** Aaron; **Johnston,** Henry; **Jordan,** Elijah; **Jordan, Jr.,** Elijah; **King,** Alfred; **King,** Peter; **Louther,** William; **Lowther,** Cupid; **McDonald,** Philip; **Overton,** Nathan; **Page,** John T.; **Paxton,** Miles; **Price,** Joseph; **Price,** Robert; **Skinner Sr.,** George; **Skinner,** Joseph; **Stewart,** Isiah; **Tatem,** Miles. There is a more extensive listing in Appendix H of Thomas Butchko's book, *"Edenton: An Architectural Portrait"*, that includes carpenters in the other townships.

Clipped from <u>Fisherman and Farmer,</u> <u>08 Feb 1889, Fri,</u> <u>First Edition,</u> <u>Page 6</u>

We are sorry to record the death of another of Edenton's most worthy colored citizens—Henry Beasly—known to all and respected for his quiet, peaceful and honest life. He died Sunday morning and was buried Tuesday. A large crowd was present at his funeral.

Clergy: Bookman, Sydney S. (CME); **Paxton**, Abram (Baptist).

Coachman

A coachman drives a horse drawn vehicle that carries people. **Alfred Blount** and **Harry Cox** (the author's great-great grandfather) were both identified as coachmen. Each could have owned or leased a coach and team, and charged people for transportation, or they could have been employed by a homeowner and used his horses and coach. In African American societies, the coachmen were among the most travelled, and the best informed. As they drove the homeowner to work, took families to church or to visit, or drove a route across eastern North Carolina, coachmen met people, exchanged information and ideas; brought back the latest news; and overheard conversations. Through this exposure to the larger world, they frequently became leaders in their communities.

Drayman

In contrast, a drayman drove a flatbed wagon with horses or mules, hauling freight, either within town, or over distances. While it was difficult work, it was a way for a freed man to start a business and make a steady living; any kind of rough wagon and a strong mule could haul lumber, tobacco, cotton, fish, crops, household goods, or trash. **Vandon Jones**, drayman, may have owned his own mule and wagon, and charged people by the load. Or he could have worked on salary for one of the mills or fisheries.

Engineer

The definition of 'engineer' in the 19th century was basically, "one who operates an engine' – such as a train, or boiler or machinery used in mills and factories. Two freedmen were identified as engineers in 1880. **Author Bonner**, age 26, is listed on the same page of the census with several "workers at saw mill," beneath the name Sam Goodwin, "mill owner." This leads us to believe Bonner, at 26, had been entrusted with the maintenance and repair of the equipment in the Goodwin mill. The other engineer was George Haughton (or Houghton) who also identified himself as a fisherman. While there is no supporting documentation, Haughton may have worked on boat engines, or equipment used in the fisheries.

Grocery Clerk: Lee, James (grocery and confectionery); **Lee,** Richard (dry goods and groceries); **McDonald, Jr.,** Philip

Harness Maker

A worker in leather, **David Harrell,** the harness maker, fashioned reins and harnesses for mules and horses that pulled the wagons, the coaches, as well as for the riding horses. He also most likely created belts, for personal and industrial use; purses, saddles, luggage, shoes, and perhaps even baseball gloves out of leather. It was heavy work, sitting at his 'stitchinghorse' bench, cutting hides with special knives; softening them with harsh chemicals, splicing, sewing and gluing the pieces into marketable items; drilling holes for rivets and fasteners, perhaps adding decorative touches, or the initials on the nicer items. By this time, Harrell was able to order the metal bits, buckles, rivets and nails he needed at a local store, or by catalog.

Hotel Cook: Jordan, Susan.

Jeweler and Gunsmith: *10-Lee, David.

Clipped from <u>Fisherman and Farmer</u>, <u>01 Aug 1890, Fri</u>, <u>First Edition</u>, <u>Page 5</u>

The party of young men from this place who went to Nags Head two weeks since on the sloop Madge, where they spent a most delightful time fishing, hunting, bathing, &c., returned yesterday morning.

D. M. Lee, one of our most enterprising and respected colored citizens, has erected a neat little shop on his lot on East Queen street, where he will soon remove his gunsmith and jewelry business. He is a man worthy the patronage of all our people.

Subscribe for your county paper. We do not say it will make you live longer and die happier, or that it will make you "solid" for a handsome obituary notice when you pass away, but it brings its own reward. Only $1.50 a year, cash in advance.

Clipped from <u>Fisherman and Farmer</u>, <u>20 Apr 1888, Fri</u>, <u>First Edition</u>, <u>Page 5</u>

R. A Caskie, senior partner of the Oyster firm here, and Miss Summie Lee, daughter of D. M. Lee, both colored, were married at the residence of the bride's father, on Monday night last, by Rev. Winfield.

Clipped from <u>Fisherman and Farmer</u>, <u>20 Nov 1891, Fri</u>, <u>First Edition</u>, <u>Page 5</u>

All persons who have things, such as Guns, Pistols, Watches, clocks and Jewelry in my shop for repairs, and have been done for weeks, are now notified to come within the next 20 days and pay for the repairs, and get them, or they will be sold for repaires, as it is the only means I have for bread, and need my money as other laborers do. Yours Truly,

D, M. LEE.

I am also prepared to do your work. I guarantee good jobs when done or no pay. Guns, Pistols, Watches and Clocks for sale. Always on hand.

NOTICE.

Having qualified as administratrix of D. M. Lee, dec'd., I hereby request all who are indebted to his estate to make immediate payment, and all who have jewelry, fire arms or any other articles in his shop for repair will call for them within the next 30 days, after which time they will be sold for repairs. All to whom the estate is indebted will present their claims within 12 months, or this notice will be pleaded in bar of recovery.

SARAH F. LEE, Adm'x.

July 7th, 1892.

Junkmen: Luten, Samuel; **Skinner**, Warren.

Laundry

Penelope Burk and ***11-Emiline Dempsey** most likely did laundry in their own yards or homes, taking in clothes and linens from others and charging by the piece. It was arduous and backbreaking work that had, almost always, been done by women. Water had to be hauled from a well or creek to the big metal wash tubs. Mrs. Burk had a couple of teen-aged sons who may have helped with the heavy hauling. The clothes were put into boiling water over an open fire, and "agitated' with a long paddle or pole. Stains were rubbed with bars of harsh soap (that may have been made at home) then scrubbed against a washboard. These women may have had "secret recipes" for removing stains, or getting linens white. Water from cooking rice and potatoes would have been used as "starch" to stiffen collars, crinolines and cuffs. Their hands, no doubt, were always red and chapped. Clothes were dried on a line, or perhaps spread on shrubs or grass to bleach in the sun. The prices they charged may have included "pressing" on a horizontal surface, or with irons that had been heated over a fire or on a stove.

We deeply regret to cronicle the extreme illness of "Aunt" Emeline Dempsy, one of the most highly respected colored women in Edenton. Her many friends, both white and colored, will doubtless read this w th sorrow.

Lumber and Sawmill Workers

BRANNING MF'G COMPANY'S ALBANIA AND PEMBROKE MILLS.

Butchko gives an extensive analysis of the development of the lumber and sawmills in his book (Butchko, p.44). After the railroad arrived in 1881, Edenton's industrial development grew and prospered. Sawmills depended on the railroads to ship finished lumber to growing markets in the north. Lumbering became Edenton's main industry. First to jump on the bandwagon was William H. Brown. Shortly after him, came Herbert H. Page. The Branning Manufacturing Company was organized in 1888, and they added another mill in 1893, expanding their holdings in Edenton. In the mid-1890s, Winborne and Rea produced decorative woodwork used on many Edenton homes.

Wilson Bembry, **Edward Blount**, **Henry Brewer**, **Richard Jerkins**, **Charles Jones**, **Samuel Jordan**, **John Kale**, **Walter Ming**, **James Price**, and **Samuel Reddick** reported their occupation as lumber and sawmill workers. Their jobs may have been to cut the limbs off of the trees, debark the logs, trimming, and planing, which is the process of smoothing the surface of the lumber.

Mattress Maker

Mattresses may have been made with feathers, straw, wool or cotton. The process of making them was basically the same, in that the stuffing material was put into a simple cotton or linen sack, called a tick. Feather mattresses were made with the feathers of geese or ducks that were being prepared for cooking. **David Blount** was the mattress maker for the town. It is not known if Edenton had a mattress-making facility, or if David Blount was doing this on his own.

Midwife

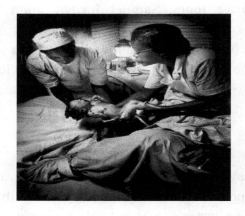

Midwifery among African American women has its history in Africa, and the knowledge and practice of delivering babies comes from generations of ancestral practice. Throughout slavery, women used what they knew and had experienced about the birth process and medical botanical roots, to deliver both babies of slaves, and the babies of the plantation owner's wife and other local white women. After slavery, the black community still needed to depend on each other's resources, and the midwife continued to be a vital resource for its health and well-being. Midwifery clinics were established for proper training. **Mary Badham** and **Fannie Skinner** listed their occupation as midwives. An excellent history of African American midwifery can be found on the website for assatashakur.org *"Black Midwives, From Africa to Now"*.

Nurse/Child's Nurse

In 1879, Mary Eliza Mahoney became the first African American professional nurse, graduating from the New England Hospital for Women and Children, in Boston. This tells us that it was recognized as a profession for which one needed training in order to safely and correctly care for people. It is not known if **Polly Cox, Charlotte Overton,** and **Milly Williams** had formal training, nor who they specifically cared for in Edenton. They might have been nurses for ill members of particular families, or even a nurse in the capacity of care for children.

Painter: Stewart, Dorsey.

Photographer

Photography was introduced to the public in 1839, mostly by Louis Daguerre in France, and William Talbot in England. Experimenters in the photographic process in the United States also started in 1839. Some photographers would travel through towns and cities, and advertise that they would hold sittings. Of course, these services were not available to African Americans yet. With the onset of the Civil War came a demand for portraits of soldiers and their families. As former slaves, and the children of former slaves began to establish themselves in their communities, the need, and hence the ability to record life's transitions and events became popular. The town photographer contributed to the fabric of community life and recorded local scenes. ***12-John Lee** and **William Sturgis** were identified as photographers. They were not natives of Edenton. Lee was born in Virginia, and Sturgis was born in New York. It is not known where they learned the trade.

Clipped from <u>Fisherman and Farmer</u>, <u>03 Feb 1888, Fri</u>, <u>First Edition</u>, <u>Page 4</u>

DEATH OF A COLORED CITIZEN.

Edenton's Photograther, John F. Lee, o: e of our most highly respected colored citizens, died at his home in this city on Thursday morning last, after a short illness. The announcement of his death, coming so unexpectedly. caused surprise and pain to many of his friends. He was a son of D. M. Lee, and was about to enter upon the 36th year of his age. He was a good man in every relation of life, a member of the A. M. E. Zion Church, kind. gentle, loving and affectionate, and while his death is a sad bereavement to his family and friends, it falls with severest effect upon the wife and three little fatherless children, to whom the sorrow and sympathies of the entire community go out in this hour of their sore affliction. He was raised in Edenton and well known by both white and colored; none knew him but to respect him.

Clipped from <u>Fisherman and Farmer</u>, <u>03 Feb 1888, Fri</u>, <u>First Edition</u>, <u>Page 4</u>

(cont'd.)

him out to respect in th.

The funeral took place from the A. M. E. Zion Church, at 3 o'clock, p. m., Friday afternoon; Rev. E. Overman, assisted by Revs. Winfield and Pindlin, conducted the service. The number of people who turned out to pay the last sad rite to his memory, attested the high esteem in which he was held.

Physician's Assistant

There were several white physicians in Edenton in 1880. ***13-Silas Miller** could have been the assistant to Cornelius Bogart (dentist), W.A.B. Norcum, Richard Dillard, Richard Dillard, Jr., George Coke, William Berkley or William J. Leary. Whether he assisted the physician in actual medical procedures, or was a personal butler is not known.

Clipped from <u>Fisherman and Farmer</u>, <u>04 Oct 1889, Fri</u>, <u>First Edition</u>, <u>Page 5</u>

Silas Miller, a colored man, of our city has received authentic information that a large fortune has been left him in California. We hope he may get it. He is a worthy man and will do good with any money he may command.

Seamstress/Dressmaker

Women who made clothes for a living may not have had the support of a male wage-earner. The fact that **Emily Haughton, Mary Johnson,** and **Mary Smith** were heads of household could have been due to divorce, or death of a spouse, or never getting married. Sewing machines were more easily available in the 1880s, so they may have had one in their homes.

Shingle Maker

Making shingles was a dangerous job that demanded a high skill level and manual dexterity. Shingle makers hand-fed pieces of wood onto an automated saw. The potential for loss of hands, fingers or arms was high. Another occupational hazard they may also have suffered from was "cedar asthma"-the lung condition resulting from breathing sawdust. This was the occupation for **Elijah Blair, Henderson Blair, David Paxton,** and **Horace Picott.**

Teachers

The earliest known public school for blacks in Edenton may have been established in 1881, a few years before Evalina Williams Badham came to head her private school in the late 1880s. This was evidenced by a deed in which five black leaders acquired a lot between Freemason and Peterson streets in 1881. One of the leaders was probably **George W. Lane**. Schools had inadequate resources, so each of the black churches sponsored a private school. The first was at St. John the Evangelist Episcopal Church in 1892. In 1895, the Edenton Normal and Industrial School was formed, through Kadesh A.M.E.; and a third school was operated by Providence Baptist Church. Approximately 75 children from almost as many families were "attending school" at the 1880 census, however, only two people reported their occupation as "teacher": **George Lane** and his wife, **Lucy Lane.** Lane was born in 1852 in Chowan County, and later attended Howard University. In 1879, he was appointed Deputy Register of Deeds for Chowan County.In 1881 he was the principal of Edenton NC Public School. It had an enrollment of two hundred scholars. Afterwards, he was made Postmaster, the first and only African American to hold this position.

Teamster

A teamster was a person who drove a horse, mule or ox-drawn freight wagon, the equivalent of the modern-day truck driver. With the increase in industry in Edenton, more products were being manufactured, and sold to distant markets, creating work for those with a wagon, and mules or oxen. It was a seven-day-a-week job, in all kinds of weather, and a self-employed teamster had little job security. During the Civil War many African-American men were employed as teamsters for the Union Army. Teamsters organized as a union in the early 20th century, and the Teamsters National Union was one of the most diverse organizations of the era. **Edmund Nixon** reported this as his occupation.

Tinner

A tinner, or tinsmith, was a handy person to have in town, because he could make and repair things made of tin, such as cups, ladles, kettles, boxes, basins and funnels.   **John W. Draper** reported this as his occupation. He also ran a stove store.

Turpentine

Samuel Simpkins made a living by harvesting turpentine from the long leaf pine trees growing in the region. Turpentine was a valuable resource, used to clean machinery, thin paint, burned as lamp fuel, and as a home remedy. During winter, Simpkins would chop deep notches in the base of long leaf pine trees. Above this, he would chip off all the bark and wood, so that the sap would seep out the bare surface, and collect in the notches. Simpkins would make his rounds, dip out the turpentine, haul it back to town and store it, until it could be distilled and sold. One had to 'tap' about 1,000 trees to make 25 barrels of turpentine. Simpkins might have been a kind of 'tenant' in the pine forest, with a long term lease from the landowner, sharing the proceeds with him, or he could have worked independently, paying a flat fee for permission to tap the trees.

U.S. Navy Sailors: Lowther, Anthony; **Rumbough,** Horace.

Watermen/Fishing/Sailors: *14-Creecy, Alfred; **Gilliam,** Atlas; **Bembury,** Lawrence; **Bennett,** Jerry; **Blair,** Joseph; **Blount,** Nelson; **Bond,** Anthony; **Clark,** William; **Gregory,** James; **Hoskins,** Thomas; **Jones,** Walter; **Kinnell,** Augustus; **Owens,** Solomon; **Paxton,** Henry; **Paxton,** Thomas; **Perkins,** Major; ***15-Reed,** Rijas (Rial in 1870, and in F&F death article)**; Skinner,** Anthony; **Spellman,** Dagman (Damon in 1870)**; Wynn,** Richard; **Wynn,** Thomas.

Clipped from <u>Fisherman and Farmer</u>, <u>16 Nov 1888, Fri</u>, <u>First Edition</u>, <u>Page 5</u>

Thursday night of last week witnessed a most brilliant marriage in high life amid colored people. Elizabeth Creecy, daughter of Alfred Creecy, and for some time a teacher in the public schools of this county, was married to Nehimiah Holley, by Rev. R. R. Walter, of Garysburg. A tremendous congregation assembled in the Baptist church (colored) to witness the ceremony, of which, were many whites with whom the bride and her family, old servants of a polite people, have ever been quite popular. We wish them happiness and return thanks for a large supply of wedding cake sent us. Baked by Jno. Wozelka, Esq., it was excellent.

Clipped from <u>Fisherman and Farmer</u>, <u>08 Jun 1894, Fri</u>, <u>First Edition</u>, <u>Page 2</u>

IN THE MIDST OF LIFE WE ARE IN DEATH

It has pleased Almighty God in his wise providence to take from our midst the soul of our esteemed and beloved Brother Alfred Creecy, who departed this life June 1st, 1894. He was born A. D., 1836, and at his death was 57 years, 10 months and 27 days. He was made a Mason October 1872, and was a member of J. R. Page Lodge, No. 13, Edenton, Chowan county, N. C. He served as Junior Deacon with honor to himself and credit to his Lodge. At the time of his death he was also in good standing with the Fraternity.

(cont'd.)

Therefore be it

RESOLVED, That we, the members of John R. Page Lodge, do sincerely mourn the loss of our Brother whom God has called from labor to reward. Be it further

RESOLVED, That we extend our deepest sympathy to the bereaved family, and that we commend them to God who is able to succor the distressed. Be it further

RESOLVED, That a copy of this be sent to the FISHERMAN & FARMER for publication, and also to the family of the deceased.

Committee on Condolence:

H. B. PETTIGREW,
ELIJAH HATHAWAY,
THOS. BEMBRY.

Clipped from <u>Fisherman and Farmer</u>, <u>30 Mar 1888, Fri</u>, <u>First Edition</u>, <u>Page 4</u>

ON ANOTHER TRIP.

Rial Reed, a colored man who for some years has lived in Edenton, and who twice occupied a prominent place on the criminal side of the trial dockets of our court, who twice went to Raleigh carrying the Sheriff with him as a special escort, and who (as he used to say, bragingly,) was "HONORABLY discharged by the State authorities," died at his home yesterday of pneumonia. Rial was among the inevitable about the market place, and will be missed notwithstanding his record. "Jesse James," among other children, is left to represent him.—Enquirer.

Chapter 3

1900

"I Will Trust in the Lord"

The late 1880s and 1890s, through the first few years of the new century was a period of strong growth in Edenton. The town's transportation systems were improved, with the arrival of the Elizabeth City and Norfolk Railroad in 1881; small industries grew into large factories, markets developed, and the beginnings of public education were established. Edenton's population more than doubled between publication of the 1870 census, and 1900. It is now populated by slightly over 3,000 people, a majority of whom are African Americans. Many freedmen from around the area, and even from Virginia and other more distant locations, were drawn to Edenton by the opportunities for work in the sawmills, lumberyards, and around the steamboats and railroads. (Butchko, p. 51)

We now find our ancestors working in the mills, steamboats, factories, and on the railroads. As draymen, they hauled goods and trash. Imagine them loading and hauling fish, cotton, grain, shingles, and lumber on and off of the trains and steamboats. They worked in the lumber and sawmills. Although Edenton had a cotton mill, none of those laborers were African American.

If your ancestor worked on the water, he did one of several things-he repaired the seine nets (seine mender/seine wright), worked on a boat, or he was a fisherman. If that was the case, he may have worked for one of five fisheries in Edenton. By 1900 however, the fishing industry had declined due to overfishing. The one and largest fishery remaining was Ed Hassell's Greenfield Fishery, one of the five fisheries that were in business in the 19th century.

65

The 1890 census is unavailable to all researchers, as it was damaged by a fire in the basement of the Commerce building in 1921, in Washington DC. Only minimal information on small areas of the country survived. Researchers have learned to live with this loss of information. Fortunately, in order to get a feel for African American life in Edenton during that time period, we can read a lot of articles from Edenton's newspaper, *Fisherman and Farmer*.

Many of those articles are in Part II of this book. While it is impossible to make an article match with every name in the census, an asterisk beside a name in this book means that I found an article about that person in the newspaper. I found my great-grandfather mentioned twice in the "Colored News" section, and a couple of other relatives as well.

There are countless writings on the history of African American life in the south. With the knowledge handed down from, and personal experiences of being treated as less than citizens economically, socially and politically--we are aware of our disenfranchisement in every facet of life. Segregation had become institutionalized, despite the promises written into law at the end of the Civil War. As tenant farmers, freedmen found it was almost impossible to pay off debts owed to white landowners, which kept them tied to the land and unable to improve their lot. Socially, we were kept away from schools, water fountains, and places of business. Politically, we were not allowed to vote. There are many places one can read for that kind of information, so in-depth commentary will not be provided here. Rather, this book wants you to take an imaginary trip into the daily lives of your ancestors, engaging your senses in what may have been the sights, sounds, and smells of Edenton in this census year, 1900.

Imagine the dawn of a new day, in late spring or summer. Our ancestors rise to the sounds of roosters crowing in backyard chicken coops, and the sounds of waking dogs barking. Men and women tell time by the sound of the bell in the courthouse cupola striking the hour. They leave their beds to dress in their simple shirts and sturdy work pants, eat breakfast and maybe pack a cold lunch of homemade bread, a slice of pork or a fresh tomato in a basket, before heading toward their places of employment. Whistles may be blowing from the mills and factories lining the waterfront and scattered around the core of the town.

 Our ancestors who were draymen brought lumber, fish, cotton, and tobacco to town on creaky wagons, and hauled trash and debris away from the busy commercial enterprises. Other ancestors worked on the two railroads that came to the waterfront. They loaded fish casks, cotton and grain; shingles, staves, turned posts, fancy Victorian woodwork and planed lumber on to trains heading north to bigger markets. They may have loaded items onto the steamboats that carried goods across the Albemarle Sound to outlying farms and communities. Their voices may have rung out in everything from conversations to call-and-response songs, field hollers, work songs, and street cries to make their day go more smoothly; and to attract customers for goods being sold from small shops and in the market. "Fresh fish fit for the pan!" "Shad! Buy any shad?" The hawking was sometimes interjected by the blowing of a tin horn, which came to be known as a fish horn. (McCutcheon, 1993. p. 136)

An ancestor listed here was a steamboat cook. Might he have been a cook on the *John W. Garrett*? That was a steamboat that carried fully loaded rail cars across the Albemarle Sound to meet up with the railroad line there. Maybe he was on the steamer *Plymouth*, which was a passenger ferry between Edenton and Plymouth on the Roanoke River. Other steamers were the *Edenton,* the *Norman L. Wagner,* and the *Haven Belle.* On July 27 of 1888, your ancestor might have been a part of the "excursion for colored people" from Edenton to Montrose; or the "large colored excursion" from Roper to Edenton on August 15, 1889, on the *Haven Belle.* A band of musicians came along also!

Sounds from the saw mills may have drowned out most others, for these were huge enterprises with dangerous equipment. The clank of the metal claws that grabbed up the ancient pine trees. The shriek as the wood was pushed into the large band saws, then trimmed and cut and fashioned into items for sale. The constant rumble as finished products were stacked and loaded for shipment rung throughout the town from the various mills.

More sights, smells, and sounds: the clanging of an anvil in a blacksmith's shop as a customer waited for his horse to be shod; the clatter of the looms through the open windows in the cotton mill, and the hammering on houses, roofs, and fences; the clip-clop of horse's hooves, and the squeak of the wheels and springs as coachmen reported to their families for whom they worked, to carry them wherever they needed to go; the lapping of the water against the wharves at the waterfront, accompanied by the sea shanty songs as the men pulled in the nets.

The town was often enveloped in a haze of acrid smoke from countless kitchen fires, train and steamboat smokestacks, and from fields being cleared by burning; maybe even from a swamp fire smoldering underground that cannot be extinguished. The smell of freshly sawn lumber, and fine sawdust permeated the town.

There was the smell of the drying fish, and the salt used to preserve them; the cloying odor of hot tar, used with oakum to seal boats; the barnyard smell from the cows, chickens and hogs kept in backyards, and the horses that pulled those wagons and coaches around town. There were the odors from privies and outhouses lining the back of many lots. The smell of flowers and fresh mown grass and hay would have been a welcome break. A handkerchief dipped in rosewater, or a few blossoms off of a lavender plant could mask some of the strong smells of life.

It was only as the sun began to set that people put down their tools, turned off the machinery, stabled the livestock, and took their rest. This was 1880s to 1900s Edenton for us.

Women were also busy, performing physical labor on roads and farms, as well as in more traditional roles. Many reported to the homes of white residents, and as servants, performed many menial tasks. They cooked, they cleaned, they washed and ironed; and they took care of children. It was by no means an easy or pretty job. They worked from fourteen to sixteen hours a day, often six or seven days a week, rarely being able to go home during those long hours and take care of their own children. Others did laundry or ironing at their own homes, for which they were paid by the piece, or they cared for the infirm or the elderly. Pay was minimal, and the ultimate disrespect was to be approached by the male head of the household, who often made advances; and expected uncontested liberties.

Hopefully you will find your ancestors among the women who were listed as washerwomen, cooks, and nurses. Think about her having to go to the back door for entry into the homes where she was employed, nursing at her breast a child who was not hers; and at the end of the long day, after the final meal, closing the kitchen, putting the children to bed, and maybe being allowed to take home leftover food. Then, returning the next morning, and the next, to do it all over again. My great-great grandmother, Priscilla Cox, endured some, if not all of this.

Forty-four types of jobs were found in the 1900 census, which completes this volume. Some of the names and occupations of African American residents can now be found in the pamphlet that was created by the Chowan County Heritage Development Council, and available at the Visitor Center in Edenton. Is your surname Price? Then maybe you are descended from Joseph or Robert Price, who were skilled artisans. Is your surname Badham? Then Hannibal, Miles, and Hannibal, Jr. may be your ancestors. They were the most well-known builders and architects in Edenton. But also remember and honor these others whose names are yours, those who are numbered in the listings of the less well-known, and the unknown, all who were trying to make life work in Edenton, North Carolina for themselves, their children and their descendants, right down to you.

The 1900 Edenton Town census had 62 pages of residents. As before, those black heads of household who were listed as farmers and laborers will be listed by what page they were on in the census. Those who had more specific occupations will be listed under the occupation. The history and explanations of some of the occupations have been detailed in the previous chapters, and for those occupations that were new in 1900, more historical detail is provided. You will enjoy continuing your research to find out more, by using the resources listed in the bibliography, visiting with elderly family and neighbors, and of course, using the internet.

One caveat in all of these names- keep in mind that these surnames are the surnames of the white residents who may have owned your ancestors at one time in history. There is no getting around that. You have your surname for that very reason. Over my years of research, I have become familiar with the original spellings of these surnames in earlier censuses, when they belonged to the white residents of Edenton. Due to census taker misspellings, spelling phonetically, or by the fact that they may have personally known the person whose name it was, and his preference for spelling his name, there may be several variations. For example, the surname Benbury may change to Bembry or Bembury. The surname Rumbough may have evolved into Rumbo. I have seen Lowther change to Louther (my ancestor was owned at one time by Tristrim Lowther Skinner), Blount to Blunt, and Henrihan to Henryhand.

Farmers and Laborers

Census Page

2. Paxton, Thomas; **Spruill**, Gilbert.

9. Bell, Robert

12. Bownes, Fred; **Morris**, Hester.

13. **Louis**, William

15. Harding, Joseph; **Lassiter**, __J__; **Powell**, James.

16. Bunch, __A__; **Cooper**, Paul.

17. Horton, Jeffrey; **Outlaw**, James.

21. Skinner, Charles

23. Shears, John

26. Harrell, S__; **Hollowell**, W__.

27. Sivells, Larry

28. Eure, Steven

29. Burt, Frank; **Felton**, Tim; **Rollings**, John.

30. Frieman, General; **Perry**, Martin.

31. Burke, William; **Cox**, Richard; **Jones**, Benbury.

32. Skinner, M__

33. Reaves, S__

37. Ellis, William

40. *16-Holly, Willis; **Jones**, James.

Clipped from <u>**Fisherman and Farmer,**</u> <u>**14 Oct 1887, Fri,**</u> <u>**First**</u>
<u>**Edition**</u>

CAUGHT IN A COTTON GIN.

Isham N. Holley, a young man of six-teen, son of Willis Holley, colored while pouring up cotton in the gin on Mr. Augustus Holley's plantation, accidently got his hand among the saws. The gin being run by steam its motion could not be stopped and ere anyone was aware of trouble the young man had his hand and forearm so badly lascerated as to require amputation. The Drs. Winborn performed the operation. Up to this writing the patient is doing well. The loss of a limb to the laboring man is by no means inconsiderable, we therefore regret this misfortune because its consequent injury is life long and irreperable. Let this, another accident among many of like character, all happening from like causes—cotton gins—be a caution to others and lead them to the exercise of prudential care in their labors around these instruments, which, though beneficial in themselves, can be so easily converted into means of torture and death.

41. Louther, H__

42. Benbury, Pilgrim

43. Bond, Fr__

44. Blunt, Hannibal

45. Newbern, Leroy; **Perkins**, Major; **Perry**, Go__.

46. Paxton, David

47. Louther, William; **Paxton**, Thomas.

48. Meltieve, John

49. Wynn, Adline

51. Edney, Joseph; **Holley**, Edward.

53. Walker, Francis; **White**, John.

61. Parker, Thomas.

Clipped from <u>Fisherman and Farmer</u>, <u>01 Mar 1889, Fri</u>, <u>First Edition</u>, <u>Page 6</u>

A very brilliant marriage, among the colored people, occurred last evening at St. John's Evangelist Episcopal church—Mr. V. D. Jones and Miss Nollie E. Cox being the contracting parties. A very large and most respectable number of invited people were present to witness the ceremony. The bride has long been a teacher of prominence in the public schools of this district and the groom is a young man of thrift and high character among the good people of both races. We wish them a full realization of every anticipated pleasure and comfort.

OUR COLORED PEOPLE.

[BY SPECIAL REPORTER]

Services at all the churches next Sunday.

James Sawyer has bought a cargo of fine oysters.

James A. Sawyer has improved his barber shop by adding a new chair and a large mirror. Sawyer believes in improvement and keeping up with the times. He deserves much credit as being a successful jack of all trades.

Bartender

Solomon Owens was a bartender, which meant he kept a bar and served drinks. It is not clear in Edenton's history whether he owned his own bar or club, or worked in a hotel where alcohol was served. Bartending is a craft, and bartenders did more than just mix drinks. They were also good listeners to their clients, and good buddies. Solomon was undoubtedly in a good position to hear about and share news among residents of the African American community. Unfortunately for Solomon, as early as 1902, the Anti-Saloon League was organizing around the state, and on New Year's Day 1909, North Carolina prohibited the sale of all alcohol.

Basket Maker: Iredell, Henry

Blacksmith: Bizzell, Rufus; **Jeanes** (?), Henry; **Skinner**, John.

Boarding House Manager

A boarding house was a building used for the purpose of allowing lodgers to rent one or more rooms for one or more nights, or sometimes for more extended periods of time. Frequently, they were family homes, where the owners took in boarders to help with the rent or payments on the house. Many African American families did this. **Henrietta Williams** was listed as the manager of a boarding house. Henrietta used her home on West Gale Street as a boarding house. She had four sons and a daughter living with her; in addition, she had nine male boarders, all of whom were employed at the saw mill; and one female boarder in the same home. (1900 census, p.23 and 24)

Brickmason/Brickyard: Bond, H__; **Bright,** William; **Freeman,** Edward; **Lowther,** J__; **Luten,** Anderson; **Luton,** Ha__; **Luton,** John A.; **Owens,** Isaac; **Powell,** Henry; **Pruden,** Thomas; **Rogers,** Henry.

Butcher: Jones, Ma__

Carpenters: Alexander, William; **Are__,** John; **Badham,** Hannibal (b. 1847); **Badham,** Hannibal (b. 1873); **Badham,** Miles (b. 1870); **Bright,** __; **Charlton,** Edward (cabinet maker); **Goodwin,** James; **Gregory,** Abraham; **Johnston,** Allen; **Jordan,** David; **Louther,** Bill; **McCraw,** Clifford; **Mews,** Miles; **Murphy,** __; **Nichols,** Henry; **Owens,** Daniel; **Page,** John R.; **Paxton,** James; **Price,** Robert; **Tatum,** Miles; **Tyler,** John; **Whidbee,** Willis.

Clergy: Cook, Samuel; **Edney,** Haywood; **Heritage,** William; *19-Knight,** Simond; **Overton,** __; **Pettigrew,** Haywood; **Riddick,** Richard; **Windfield,** Silas; **Wood,** John.

Clipped from <u>Fisherman and Farmer</u>, <u>17 Nov 1893, Fri</u>, <u>First Edition</u>, <u>Page 2</u>

OUR COLORED PEOPLE.

This column is edited by W. E. Burk.

Rev. S. P. Knight has accepted the call of the Providence Baptist church for the year of 1894 Rev. Knight is a good counselor and preacher.

Coachman: Hart, Richard.

Cotton Factory

The Edenton Cotton Mill was organized and funded in 1898. All of the first workers, for whom houses were built in the Cotton Mill Village in 1899, were white. **Robert Epps** stated that his occupation was a fireman, specifically in the cotton mill. So, although he was not employed as a cotton mill worker, it seems he worked at the cotton mill, tending or stoking the fire to the steam engines that powered the mill. The fireman fed coal or wood to the firebox, and also kept water in the boiler. As the fire heated the water, the steam created pressure, to drive the looms and other equipment.

Dock Worker: Benbury, William; **Johnston**, Malcolm

Drayman: A drayman was historically the driver of a dray, a low, flatbed wagon without sides, pulled generally by horses or mules that were used for transport of all kinds of goods. **Bazemore,** Alfred; **Brinkley,** Henry; **Burk,** Moses; **Davis,** Armstead; **Eason,** William; **Gilford,** Eli; **Green, A__; Gregory,** Henry; **Halsey,** James; **White,** Samuel.

Factory: (not specified as to which factory) **Boon,** William.

Firemen

By 1910, Edenton had four fire stations. Three were staffed by white men and one was staffed by black men. At the 1900 census, nine men cited their occupation as "fireman". The specifics of their employment were not noted, so we can't tell whether they worked at the cotton factory as Robert Epps did, or another establishment. If employed at the cotton mill, "fireman" might have meant keeping the boilers running for steam power, shoveling coal and wood at the machine room that produced power to run the looms. They may have been the beginnings of the black fire station that was located at 102 North Broad Street. They were: **Albert Creighton, Thomas Dillon, George Harden, George Harding, G__ Horton, Alexander Latham, Frank Reeves, and Henry Sawyer.**

Gardener: Cheshire, Thomas; **Howard, __; Skinner, L__.**

Hostler: A hostler was a horse groom employed at a roadside inn. **William Harris** and __ **Martin** reported this as their occupation.

Huckster: A huckster was a hawker, or street peddler who sold small wares, or farm produce. **Mi__ Phelps** reported himself as a huckster, without identifying his inventory.

Ice Factory Worker

As early as 1887, residents of Edenton began to want an ice factory. They felt that it was a "suitable place". In 1888, the editors brought up the fact that Raleigh residents had an ice factory, and described its size and horsepower. Elizabeth City's ice factory began to be discussed in 1889. Edenton town leaders continually encouraged and exhorted local businessmen to do the same. With the new year of 1891, came more exhortations to any businessman who would listen, to take up the challenge to start an ice factory. Finally, in April of 1896, the ice factory was "about completed", and would soon be in operation. By May 1 of 1896, it was up and running, and deliveries of ice were made in town, because the ice wagon had been seen. One year later, the Edenton Ice Factory had been deemed "quite a success", and was daily producing about "twenty-one tons of the purest and clearest ice you ever saw". *(Fisherman and Farmer: April 2, 1897)* One head of household, **Thomas Hawkins** specifically reported his occupation as "ice factory".

Logging: Bennett, Arthur.

Merchants: Blount, Isaac; **Lee**, Richard; **Louton**, Samuel; **McDonald**, __; **Middleton,** Joseph.

Mill/Sawmill: Austen, John; **Austin,** East; **Austin,** Joseph; **Autterbridge,** Daniel; **Bembry,** William; **Bembury,** Atlas; **Blunt,** Robert; **Bond,** Dave; **Bond,** Norfleet; **Bond,** William; **Bonner,** Mike; **Boston,** Albert (planing mill)**; Bradley,** Thomas; **Brown,** Matthew; **Burden,** Ira; **Butts,** Elijah; **Capeheart,** William; **Cox,** Eden; **Creecy,** John; **Daniels,** John; **Davis,** Walter; **Fisher,** Barral; **Gilliam,** Henry; **Gilliam,** Thomas; **Gordon,** Ca__; **H__,** Taylor; **Hassell,** Warren (fireman)**; Hathaway,** __; **Hathaway,** Mose; **Johnson,** James; **Johnson,** Thomas; **Johnston,** Nathaniel; **Jones,** Frederick; **Long,** Henry; **McLease,** David; **Pailin,** __; **Paxton,** James (engineer)**; Paxton,** William; **Perry,** Walisous; **R__,** Alexander; **Reed,** Van; **Roman,** Lewis; **Satterfield,** Richard; **Satterfield,** Thomas; **Saunders,** __; **Sherton,** John; **Silves,** Elbert; **Smith,** G__; **Thatchell,** William; **West,** William.

Nurse: Bembury, Dora; **Morris,** Mar__.

Painter: Jones, Gilbert; **West,** William

Plasterer: Norcum, John

Railroad: Askew, William; **Beasley,** Auther; **Bell,** Joseph; **Blount,** __; **Bryant,** __; **Cockram,** Peter; **Ferribo,** Richard (this surname was originally spelled Feribault, when it was the white surname in the 1800s)**; Foxwell,** Ned; **Holley,** Masoniah; **James,** Primus; **Mitchell,** Dorson; **Nelson,** Thomas; **Nixon,** Henry; **Peat,** Edward; **Reed,** Gorge; **Reid,** James; **Shapp,** Sh__sty; **Spruil,** E__; **Taylor,** __; **White,** Alexander; **Yarbrough,** Jeff.

Reaper

A reaper is a farm tool or machine for harvesting grain. The person who uses the machine is also called a reaper. **Noah Bess** and **Edward Paxton** reported their occupation as reaper. One or both of these men may have been the owner of a reaper, and gone from farm to farm, harvesting grain for others. Or they may have been employed by a farmer, and operated the reaper as part of their job.

Restaurant: Dempsey, Evalina (owner and keeper); **Lee,** Sara.

Sawyer/Lumber: Adams, Lewis; **Capehart,** John; **Capehart,** Paul; **Edny,** Edward; **Johnson,** Isaac; **Mins,** Edgar; **Spruill,** Gilbert.

Seamstress: Jones, Martha; **King**, Nancy.

Servant: Bond, E__; **Hobbs,** Hester; **Moore,** Lu__; **Williams,** Hannah; **Williams,** Hattie.

Shoemaker: Gatlin, Joseph; **Stallings,** Augustus; ***20-Tillery,** Louis.

Steamboat Cook: Beasley, Charles; **Beasley,** Jerry.

Teacher: Barclay, John; **Burke,** Maria; **Burke,** Susan; **Harris,** Sadie; **Sawyer,** Annie; **Skinner,** Cora; **Whitford,** __.

Trucker: Blunt, Henry; **Tredwill,** M__.

Undertaker

There are many excellent sources for learning about the role in the community of the African-American undertaker. **Joseph Charlton** was that person in Edenton. On death certificates, he signed his name as "E.J. Charlton". All cultures seek to bury their dead with dignity, and burial rites and traditions are as varied as the cultures that perform this rite of passage. The history of the African American burial service has its beginnings in ancient Egypt, where the practice of using cloths, spices and special preserving techniques was elaborate. During slavery, many families were not allowed the opportunity to bury their loved ones, or celebrate their lives. During the Civil War, black soldiers had the responsibility of collecting soldiers' bodies from the battlefields, and embalming and preserving them for shipment back to their homes, so they became familiar with the process. The business of funeral directors began to take hold, and elevated their role in the community. Undertakers counseled grieving families, which put them on par with clergy. In many rural towns, the dead were laid to rest in cemeteries behind churches. In Edenton during slavery, they were buried on the home plantations or the Providence burial grounds. The heretofore long-lost Providence Burial ground was finally discovered in March of 2000, and reconsecrated on February 22, 2001. Vine Oak Cemetery, also known as the "colored cemetery" had been in use throughout much of the 19th century. Concern was expressed about its upkeep in 1892 and 1893 *Fisherman and Farmer* articles.

Waiter (Hotel): Kelley, Joseph.

Waitman: Johnston, Theodore.

Wash/Iron/Cook: Beasely, Josephine; **Beasley,** Lucy; **Bembry,** Bettie; **Bembury,** Eliza; **Coffield,** __; **Cox,** Priscilla; **Davis,** Maaya; **Dempsey,** Sophia; **Eason,** Ellen; **Harrell,** M__; **Holley,** L__; **Horton,** Ch__; **James,** Ella; **Jordan,** Mary; **Lewis,** Nellie; **Moore,** Lillie; **Nixon,** Mary; **Overton,** Henrietta; **Page,** Mollie; **Pain,** Almeta; **Paxton,** Charity; **Price,** Jane; **Skinner,** Martha; **Sprout,** Maggie; **Underhill,** Nancy; **White,** Pennie; **Williams,** Ava; **Williams,** Lucinda; **Williams,** Mary; **Wyn,** Betsy.

Water/Seine/Fishing: Banks, Andrew; **Benbury,** __; **Benbury,** Samuel; **Blair,** John; **Blount,** John; **Collins,** __; **Horton,** Solomon; **Jones,** M__; **Leary,** William; **Miller,** Robert; **Moore,** Andrew; **Pain,** Att__; **Riddick,** Elliott; **Ryan,** No__; **Spruill,** Charles; **Taylor,** Sheridan; **Wynn,** Richard.

Well Digger: Felton, Martin.

Whitewasher: Granby, Walter.

Epilogue

"I Done Done Whatcha Told Me to Do"

This then, is the listing of occupations of Black heads of household in Edenton Town for the census years 1870 through 1900. Hopefully, the next volume, from the census years 1910 through 1940, will be created and printed in the not-too-distant future. Every attempt was made to include all names. For those names that were undecipherable, due to the penmanship of the census taker, I substituted lines for letters that were not clear.

Part 2 of this book has selected articles from Edenton's "Fisherman and Farmer" Colored News Section. Since the focus of this book is to document business and labor, I chose a lot of articles in those categories, although I did include other kinds of articles. They are fascinating, and give us a look into the rich and busy life in the African American community from that time period. I encourage each reader of this book to log go on the newspapers.com website, and read more about our ancestors.

I hope that this book, and the one to come, will provide information for your families that you may not have known before, answer questions about how our ancestors made that transition to full citizenship, or simply add to your knowledge about the past. It would be difficult to make every single connection of censuses to names; census data is dry and succinct. It cannot tell us of the emotions, the heartbreaks, the circuitous paths, the weight of the burdens our people shouldered. But these facts and dates validate us and our pride in our ancestors. They are proof and evidence-along with the buildings, the fields, the barns, the roads, and their strong and talented descendants that survive-that our families were there. The documentations I provided are simply jumping-off spots for your personal family journey.

You will find other documents, articles, connections, and create your own "Wow!" moments. May the ones I have shared with you here inspire a deeper look into the histories of your ancestors. But most of all, may this book help our ancestors, their stories and their contributions take a prominent and visible place in the history of this small town in eastern North Carolina. Edenton bills itself "The South's Prettiest Small Town" and our ancestors gave much of themselves to help build it. We appreciate our people and their efforts, and pray we can find similar purpose and drive, contributing to our world in ways that will bring honor to their names, and their sacrifices.

Part Two

Articles From *Fisherman and Farmer*

In this part of the book, I have selected articles from the newspaper during the years 1887-1896, the span of the years that are available at *newspapers.com,* and categorized them as follows: 1) Daily Life and People; 2) Education; 3) Entertainment and Sports; 4)Business and Labor; 5) Politics and Civics; and 6) Religion. Each category has several articles that tell a little bit about how our ancestors played a role in Edenton, whether in just our black community, or through our contributions to the town overall. Some are quaint and amusing, some are about less than savory actions by others, but life in any town is part good, and part not so good. I hope you enjoy reading the articles I chose, and hope that you will seek out more information and history on your own.

Daily Life and People

In this section are articles that mention everyday life and occurrences. Comings and goings, visitations, marriages, births, illnesses and deaths are included here. Black families took trips and excursions on some of the steamboats that went back and forth. As in any town and city, there was crime, so there were reports of criminal behavior. Families built houses, visited relatives in other states and towns, and earned positions and jobs in other places. Then there are more unusual incidents. The following articles can be found on line in the "Our Colored People" section of *Fisherman and Farmer,* on the *newspapers.com* website.

In your branch of the Overton family, is there a story in your family history about Billy, who drowned in a boating accident? Read about it the October 18, 1889 issue. Is there a story in your family history about a relative who as a child ate a partial box of lye that almost killed him or her? Read about it in the May 2, 1890 issue. An article in the November 11, 1892 paper tells of Jennie Skank, who had to kill a wild deer with an ax. It jumped her fence and she knocked it in the head. Brave woman! Finally, if you are a member of the Bembry family who likes to sing, you may have inherited that from your ancestors. The Bembry Family Quartette sang at the musical concert and poetical lecture in Hertford on Monday, April 9, 1894. They also traveled to, and sang at the Mosely Street A.M.E. Zion Church in Norfolk, VA, on May 25, 1894.

As you look into the newspaper, make sure to read the "Our Colored People" column. It is headed as "A Variety of Items Especially Interesting to that Race". There is a lot of information about the life of the community in that column. I have included individual articles, from 1888 to 1894. They were selected because of the variety of names mentioned.

Swety Leary's barber shop has again received new additions and been brightened by new touches of the painter's brush. Swety is a genius. Had he received an early training in the art of painting he would have been as good with pencil and brush as he now is with razor and scissors.

John Felton, a colored man, was seriously cut by Jim King, another colored man, on Wednesday night. King made every effort to escape the officers of the law, even tried to use his knife upon officer Leary but, was soon mastered and safely ensconced in the County prison where he awaits the consequences of his unlawful deed. When the officer found the prisoner he was hid in a house near the Woodard wharf. He

Clipped from <u>Fisherman and Farmer</u>, <u>16 Nov 1888, Fri</u>, <u>First Edition</u>, <u>Page 5</u>

(cont'd.)

ran from thence in the water whence the officer persued him. In the water he showed great desperation cutting at the officer several times. Finally by the assistance of colored citizens, anxious for the law's vindication, the offender was overcome. The wounded man's condition is considered serious. Much speculation is indulged as to final consequences. We have not learned the cause of the assault but, from all that now appears, it must have been a wauton and malicious attack.

Clipped from Fisherman and Farmer, 23 Nov 1888, Fri, First Edition, Page 6

The colored man, John Felton, who was so severely cut in the difficulty reported by us last week, is greatly improving. We were invited to witness the dressing of his ugly wounds by Dr. Leary on Friday. There are three gashes, making almost a circuit of the shoulder-arm of the stout man, each of which, appear to be healing and doing well.

Clipped from Fisherman and Farmer, 07 Dec 1888, Fri, First Edition, Page 6

James King, the colored man who cut John Felton, also colored, of which mention has been heretofore made by us, upon failure to give bond in the sum of two hundred dollars for his appearance at the next term of the Superior Court for Chowan, was committed to prison on Friday.

Clipped from <u>Fisherman and Farmer</u>, <u>08 Mar 1889, Fri</u>, <u>First Edition</u>, <u>Page 6</u>

Jim Moore, colored, said on the evening of the 4th, "Well, good times is come at lass. Harrison have gone to de White House to-day and I am going to bed to-night." On being asked if he had not been going to bed every night, said "No, and if Harrison had not went to the White House I would not'er went to bed at all." This man has been staying at Miller's restaurant for eight months and has refused to go to bed till the night of the 4th. Hope he slept well.

Clipped from <u>Fisherman and Farmer</u>, <u>18 Oct 1889, Fri</u>, <u>First Edition</u>, <u>Page 5</u>

Boat Capsized and One Man Drowned.

Monday night the Sloop Annie Colton. in crossing the Albemarle sound, capsized. One of the only two men, colored, aboard was drowned Billy Overton, a son of Elder Overton of the A. M. E. Zion church. William Pratt was taken from the sloop's bottom by the Str. Roberts. Tuesday morning, while en route from Columbia to Edenton.

Overton held to the sloop as long as he could but, giving out in strength and hope about four o'clock Tuesday morning, he turned loose and was seen no more.

Clipped from <u>Fisherman and Farmer</u>, <u>15 Nov 1889, Fri</u>, <u>First Edition</u>, <u>Page 4</u>

NOTICE.

The mother of William Overton, the drowned boy who was one of the crew of the "Annie Colton" capsized on the 15th. of last month, desires any information leading to the recovery of her son's body. Parties hearing or, seeing anything that would likely lead to its recovery would confer a great favor by communicating at once to Alice Overton Edenton, N. C.

Clipped from Fisherman and Farmer, 13 Dec 1889, Fri, First Edition, Page 4

One of our worthy colored men, John Capehart, is erecting a very desirable dwelling on East Gale street. The sober, industrious color-ed man, in this country, is bound to succeed. There is nothing to pre-vent it, if only his health is spared him and he is content to be an hon-est, respectful and obedient citizen observing law and order.

Clipped from Fisherman and Farmer, 27 Dec 1889, Fri, First Edition, Page 1

R. M. LEE,

a colored man, well known in this community is a marvel to every one He would indicate by his present surroundings that he was of that class in business life who were "never born to die." Dick is like a cork, he'll come up, no matter how many times you sink him At

R. M. Lee, one of our most successful colored merchants, recently sustained quite a heavy loss by fire. It seems that Sunday night he put his box of money, some $500, in the stove for safety. The next morning before he had gotten out of bed his child had started fire in the said stove, and he appeared just in time to save only a small portion of the burning cash· Dick says he is not broke but continues to "get there" all the same.

Clipped from <u>Fisherman and Farmer</u>, <u>09 May 1890, Fri</u>, <u>First Edition</u>, <u>Page 5</u>

Matrimonial.

Married in Edenton, on May 1st. N. W. Ryan, Esq. to Miss M. J. Satterfield. The groom is one of our leading colored citizens, is extensively engaged in fishing, and displays business energy and a marked courtesy which merits for him the negard in which he is held. His bride has by systematic study acquired a degree of attainment which makes her esteemed by her associates. The ceremony was performed by the Rev. S. P. Knight, and the marriage took place at the residence of the bride's father. To attest their kind feeling for the contracting parties several of the leading white citizens of the town were among the donors of presents upon the accasion, and the number of presents given by friends, white and colored, was a substantial evidence of the good wishes of our people for the future happiness of the married couple.

Clipped from <u>Fisherman and Farmer</u>, <u>02 May 1890, Fri</u>, <u>First Edition</u>, <u>Page 5</u>

Edenton yesterday.

The sound of the saw and hammer is still on the air. Improvements are noticable in all parts of our city.

One call will send a man to put out a fire, but it takes half a dozen calls to make him get up and start one.

A colored child living on King street, ate about one-third of a box of lye on yesterday which came near resulting in death.

Miss Narcissa Sawyer who has been visiting her sister, Mrs. L. F. Ziegler, in this town, left yesterday for her home at E. City.

The "C" Social given by the ladies this week, at the Opera House, for the benefit of the Baptist Parsonage, was indeed a success. The proceeds were

Clipped from Fisherman and Farmer, 06 Jun 1890, Fri, First Edition, Page 5

Died at Baltimore one day last week of consumption Miss Lottie Harper, one of the colored public school teacher of this town. She was indeed a good woman. a smart and intelligent scholar and one that was universally respected In her death the colored portion of our community has lost a most faithful and dilligent worker. We extend our sympathy to the bereaved·

Clipped from Fisherman and Farmer, 15 Aug 1890, Fri, First Edition, Page 5

The old faithful street hand, Anderson Harrell, colored, who for the past five years drove the trash cart in our city. is no longer to be seen. He died Sunday morning last. He was a faithful servant, a good man and. commanded the respect of all. Peace to his ashes!

Clipped from <u>Fisherman and Farmer</u>, <u>03 Oct 1890, Fri</u>, <u>First Edition</u>, <u>Page 5</u>

Wild fowl innumerable and of every variety abound in the waters of the Sound, Bay, rivers and creeks, while 'possums, coons, squirrels, quail and deer may be found within a few miles of Edenton.

The escape of a prisoner, Spence Felton, on Tuesday evening last, was one the excitements about the Court House. He was chased by the Sheriff and others but soon took the woods. $50 reward is offered for him.

Among the visiting Attorneys here this week in attendance of Court are Messrs R. W. Winborne, of Murfreesboro, J. H. Sawyer, of E. City, W. B. Shaw, of Shawboro, C. L. Pettegrew, of Plymouth. Hon. T. G. Skinner, of

$50 Reward

FOR ONE

Spencer Felton, col'd.,
AN ESCAPED PRISONER !

Spencer Felton is about 5 ft. high, Black eyes, hair and hide, small side whiskers and mustache, weight about 125 or 130 lbs., bench legged and slue footed, when seen last was dressed in blue coat and striped pants. black slouch hat. white shirt and collar. wearing a ''barber's'' scarf pin on left lappell of coat.

J. H. PERRY, Sheriff,
Edenton N. C.

Clipped from <u>Fisherman and Farmer</u>, <u>17 Oct 1890, Fri</u>, First Edition, Page 5

Spence Felton, the escaped prisoner, has been caught and placed in Edenton Jail for safe keeping. He was captured at Gum Neck, Tyrrell county, by a M. Fred Patrick, who brought him to this city on Monday and demanded the $50 reward, which Sheriff Perry willingly paid him.

Clipped from <u>Fisherman and Farmer</u>, <u>11 Nov 1892, Fri</u>, First Edition, Page 8

Tuesday last Mrs." Jennie Skank living about 3 miles from town, killed a wild deer with an ax, It jumped the fence and fell and she knocked it in the head.

Clipped from <u>Fisherman and Farmer</u>, <u>23 Mar 1894, Fri</u>, <u>First Edition</u>, <u>Page 2</u>

The Bembry Quartette sang at Kedesh church last Sunday evening. Their music was very fine and filled the whole church with perfect enchantment. A volunteered contribution was given them of $6.56.

Clipped from Fisherman and Farmer, 13 Apr 1894, Fri, First Edition, Page 3

The Musical Concert and Poetical Lecture at Hertford last Monday night by Edenton talent surpassed their advertisement. The music rendered by the Bembry Family Quartette was grand, while the Poetical lecture delivered by Prof. R. M. Lee was far beyond his past record. Amidst cheers and applause he delivered 208 verses of his own production without manuscript, subject: "Divinity of Christ." There was a nice audience present and in addition to the admission there was a volunteered collection given. We thank the good people of Hertford for their patronage and hospitality.

Education

The earliest known public school for blacks in Edenton seems to be evidenced by a deed in which five black leaders acquired a lot between Freemason and Peterson streets in 1881. One of the leaders was probably George W. Lane. Lane was born in 1852 in Chowan County, and later attended Howard University. In 1879, he was appointed Deputy Register of Deeds for Chowan County. In 1881 he was the principal of Edenton NC Public School. It had an enrollment of two hundred scholars. Afterwards, he was made Postmaster, the first and only African American to hold this office in the town. In 1875, Evalina Williams who became the wife of carpenter Hannibal Badham, came to Edenton from New York, along with another teacher, Lotta Harper, to teach local blacks. Her husband built her school in the late 1880s.

From that point through the early 1890s, the Colored Public School was mentioned in the newspaper several times. Each of the black congregations later established their own schools. The first to do so was St. John the Evangelist Episcopal Church in 1892; followed by the inception of the Edenton Normal Industrial High School/College in 1896 under the auspices of Kadesh A.M.E.Z. Church. Finally, Providence Baptist Church opened their school in 1908.

Entered at the Post Office at Edenton as Second-Class Matter.

Scales and Plants.

Several new buildings are going up in Edenton.

Our Public (colored) School will open December 5th.

Cleveland French Dips can be found this week at Hayes'.

Edenton's future looks bright. Everything indicates a boom.

Bertie Court was in session last week. Court at Manteo this week.

Boston milk stews, at Hayes' Oyster Saloon, only 25 cents.

J. P. Hettrick shipped two boxes of

Clipped from Fisherman and Farmer, 06 Jan 1888, Fri, First Edition, Page 5

On Tuesday evening last the colored School house, in the upper part of the town, took fire from the flue, and had it not been for some one passing who discovered it before the flames got under full headway, the building would doubtless have been distroyed. The scholars all did good work and soon put it out.

Clipped from <u>Fisherman and Farmer</u>, <u>27 Jan 1888, Fri</u>, <u>First Edition</u>, <u>Page 5</u>

cold as blazers.

Mrs. O. Newman is opening a Ladies Dress Store, on Main Street, next to the FISHERMAN & FARMER Office.

Newspaper borrowers, says an exchange, find more fault with a paper than those who subscribes and pay for it.

The entertainments given every Friday night at the colored school house, by the pupils, are very interesting.

Not a girl in Edenton has availed herself of the opportunity of Leap Year, so far as we have heard. Boys, be patient.

Shopping in town this week has been immense, and it was a pleasant sight to see the crowds pouring in and out of the stores.

Clipped from <u>Fisherman and Farmer</u>, <u>07 Mar 1890, Fri</u>, <u>First Edition</u>, <u>Page 5</u>

The hotels have been crowded this week with drummers and other visitors.

This is fine pneumonia weather. Better be careful during this damp spell.

The colored public School in Edenton is in a flourishing condition.

Travelling salesmen, with Spring Samples, are daily seen in our midst.

Quite a noticeable change took place in the temperature when March came in.

Clipped from <u>Fisherman and Farmer</u>, <u>04 Apr 1890, Fri</u>, <u>First Edition</u>, <u>Page 5</u>

We are glad to learn that the Colored Public School is doing more efficient work this session than it has done for a long time. We do not have the fighting and so much disorder on the streets as we have formerly seen. This is saying a great deal for the discipline of the school.

We learn that there are two pure blood ed Africans in our town who are from the Congo section They are students at Shaw University, Raleigh. who were sent over by Miss Lula C. Fleming, a graduate of Shaw who is a missionary in the employ of the mission Union, Boston, Mass. These gentlemen will exhibit African curiosities and lecture on the manners and customs of their people. They lectued at the Colored Bap tist church last night and will lecture to night at the A. M. E. Zion church. The proceeds are to go towards defraying their expenses at school· There is no doubt of there being pure Africans. Their teacher Mr. S. N. Vass, of Shaw, is with them· Their ages respective are 19.

COLORED PUBLIC SCHOOL:

The colored Public School is located on West Freemason St. It is a one story structure containing two rooms.

Nothing but first grade teachers were employed in this school during its last session. It has the largest attendance, without any exception, of any school in the county. The results of the school have been highly satisfactory under the care of Mr. W. J. Heritage and his efficient assistants who were Mrs. E. L. Badham, Miss Lottie Harper, deceased, and Miss Nellie E. Jones.

Besides the above, there are several private schools, for both races, in Edenton and all in a most flourishing condition

Clipped from Fisherman and Farmer, 17 Apr 1891, Fri, First Edition, Page 5

The change in the weather has made quite a change in the Colored Public School in Edenton. Last week this school had about three hundred and forty scholars: this week, we are told, there are only about one hundred and sixty in attendance.

The colored public school ended its session on the 24th of April with public examination and other appropriate exercises at the school house. Last night, the 30th, the scholars gave an exhibition at the Opera House. They all rendered their selections with credit to themselves and showed that the teachers have not spared any pains in their efforts to guide their scholars in the right way. We cannot say too much for the efforts put forward by the Principal and his assistants to raise this school to a bases corresponding with our best schools. Just here we would remind our colored people of the important fact that they ought to arouse themselves and give their teachers better facilities for doing good work by tearing down the old school building and constructing another which would be a credit to them and the town.

Education! The colored people of this county will be called upon during the month of July to take in consideration the establishment of a college in this county for the education of the youth. Watch the Fisherman & Farmer for information from time to time.

At a meeting of the school committee of Edenton District the following teachers were employed to teach the ensuing term: Prof. W. J. Herritage, principal, Mrs. E. H. Badham, Mrs N. E. Jones, Mrs S. J. Burton. Educate your children and you'll make them good men and women

Colored Industrial School.

Our colored people have established in this city an Industrial High School, which opened
on the 6th inst. with an enrollment of fourteen students. Since
hat time the list has increased
daily—forty-eight now being the
number enrolled—representing
three counties. Another teacher
will soon be employed. We wish
the school success.

Entertainment and Sports

As Edenton grew, there were more opportunities for residents to engage in social activities. Churches and schools in both the black and white communities provided musical concerts, socials and excursions on the steamboats. Private teachers gave instrumental and vocal instruction.

In 1888, Edenton hosted the Black Diamond Quartette, natives of Raleigh, NC, who traveled the region, singing in several cities. They were billed as being "composed of a number of leading local colored artists" in the Baltimore Sunday Herald newspaper. Their given names were D.F. Hooper, John Taylor, Robert Curry, and Henry Wise.   They had an additional part to the group's name, "and Combination", which makes it seem as if there were other men in the group. Each member of the quartet sang a solo, but there was also a man by the name of Charles Boston, who had one leg, and was described as the "only one-legged song and dance man and plantation wing dancer". Since the "wing" step typically called for hopping on one leg, and shooting out the other to form a wing shape, Charles Boston must have been something to see! When they came to Edenton on May 18 of 1888, it was for a concert to benefit the Colored Orphan Asylum, established in 1883 in Henderson, North Carolina. In 1899, the Staunton Spectator (Staunton, Virginia) had an article about them. They also performed at the Laird Opera House in Pennsylvania in December of 1901. They may have adopted stage names, because they were now "Bad Luck Jones", "Tangle Foot Charlie" (the singer with one leg), "Bill Shines" and "High Ball Harry".

Another group, the Blind Singers, was composed of four men. They had been to Edenton in about 1881, and came back in 1889 to sing at the "colored" churches, while the Bembry Quartette continued to impress their listeners.

Strike up the band! Edenton also had talented instrumentalists. How they learned to play is not known. What we do know is that the Edenton Star Band was organized in the early 1880s. It is not known where they performed, but they possibly played at church gatherings and celebrations in the black community. Later, the "Quicksteps" brass band became the band of the Quicksteps baseball team, which was a part of the sports scene.

There were two baseball clubs, each with their own band. First, the Edenton Star Baseball Club which was formed in the 1880s, and their band; followed by the Quicksteps baseball club, with their band.

In 1888, the Star baseball club was the "colored Base Ball Club", and played against the Club of Williamston, after receiving a challenge. The Star baseball club won, and from that point on, the two Edenton teams were an integral part of sports entertainment, achieving national recognition, and support from their hometown.

Clipped from <u>Fisherman and Farmer</u>, <u>15 Jun 1888, Fri</u>, <u>First Edition</u>, <u>Page 5</u>

The colored Base Ball Club of this place received a challenge this week from the Club of Williamston and will play a match game of ball on Monday next, June 18th, in Edenton. Everybody invited to be present.

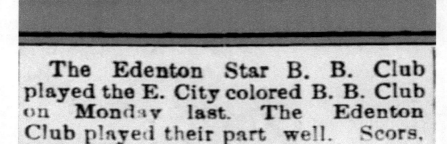

The Edenton Star B. B. Club played the E. City colored B. B. Club on Monday last. The Edenton Club played their part well. Scors, Edenton 5, E. City 0.

WANTED—To employ a man, mule and cart. A reliable and industrious man may contract for regular employment and a lot for a home. Apply at this office.

The Edenton Graded School will

Clipped from <u>Fisherman and Farmer</u>, <u>11 Jan 1889, Fri</u>, <u>First Edition</u>, <u>Page 6</u>

The four excellent Blind Singers, (colored) who appeared before an Edenton audiance some eight years since, are again in our midst. They are giving nightly concerts at the colored churches, and large crowds attend.

A Rare Musical Treat.

The management of the Young Men's Christian Association has provided a rare musical treat for our people' who love good music and don't object to a good laugh with it. They have engaged the Black Diamond Quartette to give one of their unique and most enjoyable entertainments Thursday night at the Opera-House. These four remarkable singers are colored men from Raleigh, N. C., who sang last night and the night before at the Augusta street Methodist Church to large and delighted audiences. Simmons, the leader, is a veritable black diamond with a bass voice that is the deepest we have ever heard. The other three are superb in their parts—one having a voice like a woman. The song "You had better quit your meanness" (Sam Jones) is alone worth more than the admission, which is only a quarter, and the chorus, "You can't cross here," is hard to beat. Simmons is also a fine banjoist and gives some good accompaniments on the organ. The entertainment is varied and attractive, and some of our best judges of music, who have heard them, highly endorse the Quartette. Reserved seat tickets for sale at Olivier's.

Clipped from <u>Fisherman and Farmer</u>, <u>11 Jan 1895, Fri</u>, <u>First Edition</u>, <u>Page 3</u>

THE COLORED QUAR-TETTE.

The colored Quartette of this place sang at E. City last week. The *Carolinian* speaks of them as follows:

"Having heard of the peculiar musical talent of the "Benbury Family," of Edenton, we attended one of their Concerts at the Corner Stone Baptist Church here last week, and we confess it was an hour enjoyably spent.

Clipped from <u>Fisherman and Farmer</u>, <u>11 Jan 1895, Fri</u>, <u>First Edition</u>, <u>Page 3</u>

(cont'd.)

There are four of them, two broth ers and two sisters, and their singing is unique—entirely different from any we had ever heard. While it cannot be styled "scientific" music, it is charmingly melodious to the ear.

the fence this week and cries to the top of his voice, "Office!" Does the Republicans want him?

Quite a number of our merchants will go North next week to purchase Fall Stocks. The prospects were never better for a big Fall trade,

A crack colored Base Ball Club of Elizabeth City came up Tuesday to play the Edenton boys, who licked them decently. We are told that the E. City Club failed to make a round.

The speech of J. W. Draper, at the Republican County Convention on Saturday last, was the best we have ever heard John make. It was full of good sense from beginning to end.

Two of the largest tomatoes we have ever seen were brought us this week by this week on the ice.

Rev Blount Wynn was badly hurt Monday at the Rapers mill by falling from the upper story.

The instruments of the Edenton Quickstep Band have arrived. Now for music, boys. Get a good teacher and you'll be strickly in it.

Don't quarrel with the white people because of our condition, for it is our own fault. When we make money we fail to take care of it.

Clipped from <u>Fisherman and Farmer</u>, <u>24 Feb 1893, Fri</u>, <u>First Edition</u>, <u>Page 8</u>

be will remain for some time.

Miss Mattie Mabin paid our city a flying visit on Sunday last.

Easter Sunday in this section is becoming to be one of our greatest days.

Edenton will soon have another Brass Band. making two colored bands.

Messrs W. R. Capehart and S. W. Lewton have been sick for the past few days.

Two of Edenton's fair daughters will enter into matrimony next month.

Clipped from <u>Fisherman and Farmer</u>, <u>27 Apr 1894, Fri</u>, <u>First Edition</u>, <u>Page 3</u>

pleasing.

Prof. R. M. Lee, who has been off on a lecturing tour, returned yesterday, reporting a successful trip.

The Quickstep Brass Band is improving, and the boys are now rendering some fine selections. They deserve praise.

The lecture by Rev. O. G. Jenkins last Monday night at Kedesh church was greatly enjoyed by all present.

A big Fair will be held at the

Entrepreneurship and Labor

Economic independence has been the goal of African Americans long prior to the Civil War, and up to this present day. Slaves and free blacks sought to develop enterprises to better their condition, and the names are endless. Some of the better known national historical entrepreneurs include Paul Cuffe, a sea captain; Clara Brown, an ex-slave who established a laundry and bought real estate; Maggie Lena Walker, the first woman to charter a U.S. bank; Madame C.J. Walker, manufacturer of hair care products for African American women and one of the first American women millionaires; and current-day entrepreneurs such as Robert Johnson, the creator of BET (Black Entertainment Television); Wally Amos, founder of "Famous Amos" chocolate chip cookies; and Oprah Winfrey, who needs no introduction.

Edenton had its share of black entrepreneurs, in addition to those who labored in the other businesses of the town, all helping to provide make the town a community that provided a variety of services and products to its residents, and contributing to its growth. When the "Our Colored People" column was incepted in July of 1891, it promoted those who had businesses. Are you a Leary descendant? Two of the more successful and prominent residents noted in Edenton's history were Josephine and Sweety Leary. Detailed information about their buildings can be found in Butchko's book. Josephine and Sweety were barbers who invested in real estate and used their building as rental property. They were former slaves. Mrs. Leary repaired her barbershop on "Cheapside" in 1892, but in 1893, every structure on Broad Street from King to Water Street burned to the ground.

It was rebuilt in 1894, this time with an elaborate Victorian metal front which was the most modern of building types, and believed to be fireproof. Mrs. Leary's name and the year 1894 are stamped into the front of her building, the largest of the metal front structures, covering three lots on Edenton's main street.

Other businesses were blossoming. Aches and pains? Try Samuel Luton's Buck Horn Liniment. Need a shave? Go see Mr. T.S. West. Mrs. Lee served oysters in any style. Groceries, toys, general merchandise, barbershops, shoemakers and dressmakers-- all were a part of the economic fabric of Edenton. In 1893, it was reported that Edenton had "32 places of business owned and run by colored people", and they were all doing good business, generating income and being recognized as upstanding, important contributors to the betterment of the town.

For those who did not own a business, their business was to report to work at the various lumber, saw and planing mills, cotton gins and mills, railroad yards, shipyards and fisheries that came to Edenton as the industrial revolution finally reached the south.

These jobs had their dangers. There are reports of a fire at a blacksmith's shop, and several reports of losses of limbs at the various gins and mills. Tragically, some accidents led to death, as in the case of Rev. Blount Wynn, of Providence Baptist Church. He apparently was not a pastor at Providence, as his name is not listed among the historical pastors of the church. He may have been an associate pastor. Rev. Wynn worked at the Ropers mill and on January 23, 1893, fell from the upper story. He died several days later as a result of his injuries.

Clipped from Fisherman and Farmer, 07 Oct 1887, Fri, First Edition, Page 1

Among the many arrivals in our town this week we note, Hon. H. A. Gilliam, Hon. M. L. Eure, Hon. Wm. P. Roberts. Hon. T. G. Skinner, distinguished men who, though not old, form a happy and able connection between the past and present.

Henry James (colored,) not appreciating the danger, stored fodder in a portion of his blacksmith shop which, on Tuesday, caught fire from a spark emitted by the forge, consuming the building and somewhat damaging two other houses adjacent thereto.

Remember the Fair at E. City will be held on the 18th, 19th and 20th of this month. Parties who wish to spend the whole time there will do well to stop at the Restaurant of Chas. Williams, corner of Poindexter and Main streets, where everything will be found nice

Clipped from <u>Fisherman and Farmer</u>, <u>27 Apr 1888, Fri</u>, <u>First Edition</u>, <u>Page 5</u>

We would advise all who want their pictures taken not to delay, but go at once while the prices are cheap which lasts only a few days longer, at Murphy's Gallery, opposite the Post Office.

At Skinner's Point Fishery, on Monday last, a young colored man, named Tob Cabarrus, fell from the steamer while putting out the seine and was drowned. At this writting he has not yet been found.

Murphy, the artist, is doing good work. He has made and delivered, from April 3d to date 210 Photographs and 362 Ferrotypes, which is excellent for only three weeks and a proof that satisfaction is given.

right place" and does his work well.

Little Emma. infant daughter of Mr. J. K. and Mrs. Maggie G. Rea was baptised at the M. E. church by Rev. Earnest Stevens on Sunday last.

A colored man, Milford Dicks, was taken with sun stroke while at work at Branning's mill on Wednesday evening and died before reaching home.

Mrs. Owens. the woman who murdered her husband at Creswell and who was sent to the State prison. died there last Friday with heart disease.

Mr. H. A. Bond, Sr., and his ac-

Clipped from Fisherman and Farmer, 15 Nov 1889, Fri, First Edition, Page 5

Jno. Clarke, of color, while at work in the gin-house of Mr. A. A. Perry, near Edenton, accidentally got his right hand caught in the saws of the machine which lascerated his fingers to an extent that required their immediate amputation.

Clipped from Fisherman and Farmer, 28 Nov 1890, Fri, First Edition, Page 5

to Baltimore this week to purchase a large display of Christmas goods. Look-out for his grand opening next week.

WANTED AT ONCE.—One or more good loads of hard wood from some delinquent subscriber. Those who havn't wood can bring something else.

A colored man named Riddick Sanders had his hand caught in the cotton gin of Mr. Willis Jordan last week and so badly mashed that it had to be amputated.

Because a man parts his hair in the middle, it does not necessarily follow that he is a man of many parts. This may be necessary to keep him evenly balanced.

Thanksgiving services were held in the Baptist and Episcopal churches on

Clipped from <u>Fisherman and Farmer</u>, <u>15 Jan 1892, Fri</u>, <u>First Edition</u>, <u>Page 4</u>

funeral of Rev. Abraham Mabin on Sunday next.

This column will soon be marked with too more marriages. Watch this column.

The Edenton Laundry has removed to the residence of D. M. Lee on Queen street.

The girls have commenced to celebrate leap year by presenting the boys with hat marks.

Rev. M. N. Levy will fill his pulpit on Sunday next. All are invited,

Clipped from <u>Fisherman and Farmer</u>, <u>13 May 1892, Fri</u>, <u>First Edition</u>, <u>Page 8</u>

is visiting relatives and friends in this city.

Great many will leave for Plymouth next week to attend the Association.

Messrs. Blount & Lee have opened a first class Ice Cream Saloon on Broad street.

Glad to see Messrs D. M. Lee and Thos Hawkins out again after a few days of sickness.

Mr Whitaker Reeves was badly hurt at the mill one day last week.

Clipped from <u>Fisherman and Farmer</u>, <u>20 May 1892, Fri</u>, <u>First Edition</u>, <u>Page 8</u>

Miss Lizzie Henryhand is doing some noble work in the mission field.

Our town has been made very lively this week with passing strangers.

Mr. C. S. Skinner, Jr., has opened a restaurant on East side of Broad street.

Grand picnic at Athel on the 24th. A concert at night at Pleasant Grove church.

Messrs. C. C. Manning and J H. Halsey returned from Norfolk on

Clipped from <u>Fisherman and Farmer</u>, <u>27 May 1892, Fri</u>, <u>First Edition</u>, <u>Page 8</u>

at E. City.

Rev J. C. Edney returned Monday reporting fine success with his grand rally on Sunday last. Amount raised $73.48.

Jacob Skinner is still making some fine ice cream. Jake is a hustler and deserves success He can beat them all on candy.

Misses Mariah Burke, Julia Capehart and Sophia Valentine came home from Estey Seminary at Raleigh on the 21st.

The G. A. R. Harrell Post No.

(cont'd.)

(cont'd.)

Clipped from <u>Fisherman and Farmer</u>, <u>11 Nov 1892, Fri</u>, <u>First Edition</u>, <u>Page 8</u>

(cont'd.)

Clipped from <u>Fisherman and Farmer</u>, <u>02 Dec 1892, Fri</u>, <u>First Edition</u>, <u>Page 8</u>

town a flying visit this week on business.

The Baptist Pilot has moved from Winton to Litt'eton. May it live long.

Mr Samuel World had his leg badly mashed at the mill last Saturday evening.

The Baptist Sunday School is making big preparations for the Christmas service.

Rev C. M. Cartwright has tendered his resignation to Mt. Zion Bap—

Clipped from <u>Fisherman and Farmer</u>, <u>27 Jan 1893, Fri</u>, <u>First Edition</u>, <u>Page 8</u>

this spring for New Haven, Conn. Nothing like it boys.

Messrs James Costen and Moses Miles came to Edenton from Roper this week on the ice.

Rev Blount Wynn was badly hurt Monday at the Rapers mill by falling from the upper story.

The instruments of the Edenton Quickstep Band have arrived. Now for music, boys. Get a good teacher and you'll be strickly in it.

Don't quarrel with the white peo—

Clipped from <u>Fisherman and Farmer</u>, <u>10 Feb 1893, Fri</u>, <u>First Edition</u>, <u>Page 8</u>

Providence Baptist Church loses another one of its faithful members. Rev. Blount Wynn departed this life on the 3rd at his home on East Albemarle street. His death was the result of the fall he received at Raper's mill on Jan 23rd. A good man gone to rest. Weep not.

The funeral of Rev B'ount Wynn took place in Providence Baptist Church on Sunday evening last. The church was filled to such an extent that it was impossible to seat the congregation The sermon preached by Rev S. P. Knight was an excellent one.

___

house to see Doggett & Burk.

Some newspapers seem to think the colored people are where they were 3 years ago. Not so, they are progressing rapidly.

Among the business places in our town there are 20 stores, 6 restaurants, 3 barber shops and 5 shoe shops run by colored people.

Have you visited the new store of J. E. Capehart & Son on Granville st? If not call on them; they can please you in fine groceries.

Mrs Martha A. Oden, of Washington county, is visiting in our city

Miss Nellie Chesson of Mackeys Ferry spent a few days in our town this week.

Mr John Miller had his hand badly mashed at the N. & S. depot while coupling cars.

Don't borrow your friend's paper. Subscribe for it. It will cost you only 75c for six months.

Mr Jack Bembery has on exhibition nine fine quails at his place on

---

Mrs. Betsev Sawyer,
DRESSMAKER,

who can please you in first class work and the latest sty'es. You will do well by calling on her. Prices to please you. East Albemarle street.

I am now prepared to do all kind of repairing on Boots and Shoes also repairs on 'amps. Call and see me

W. F. Skinner & Co.
Shoe shop on Queen St.

Clipped from <u>Fisherman and Farmer</u>, <u>07 Apr 1893, Fri</u>, <u>First Edition</u>, <u>Page 8</u>

church was greatly enjoyed by all present.

Prof W. J. Herritage went to E. City Tuesday to attend the Masonic celebration.

Mr E. D. Skinner had his hand badly cut with a saw at the mill on Saturday last.

It is now law for everybody to attend to their own business and let others alone.

Go to E. L. Brinkley's for a first class fitting suit—made to order.

Clipped from <u>Fisherman and Farmer</u>, <u>28 Apr 1893, Fri</u>, <u>First Edition</u>, <u>Page 8</u>

will convene at E. City on Tuesday May 23rd.

Mr. David Thompson of Plymouth was in our town last week on his way North.

Master Dink Paxton had his fingers cut off last Thursday at the planing mill.

Mr S. S. Lane was married on the 20th to Miss Alexzina McClenny both of Washington county.

Miss Robertie Forton of Hertford is delighting her many friends in this

Clipped from <u>Fisherman and Farmer</u>, <u>15 Sep 1893, Fri</u>, <u>First Edition</u>, <u>Page 8</u>

Mr. Alfred Creecy has made a pair of trucks which he says he can move a house that it will take fifteen men to move, with only three men. If you want a house moved cheap give him a call.

Edenton has 32 places of business owned and run by colored people, in this number there are 11 groceries, 6 resturants, 2 confectionery stands, 3 barber shops, 7 shoe shops, 1 bar room and 1 pool or billiard room. All are doing fairly good business.

OYSTERS.

Having opened a first-class

Oyster Saloon

at the old tin shop stand on Broad street, I invite the patronage of the people, promising to spare no pains to satisfy my customers. Oysters served in all styles, at low prices. and at all hours.

SARAH LEE.

Clipped from <u>Fisherman and Farmer</u>, <u>26 Jan 1894, Fri</u>, <u>First Edition</u>, <u>Page 3</u>

Luton's Buck Horn Liniment is
    still in the lead,
To verify the same his advertise-
    ment read;
No aches or pains seldom abide,
When Buck Horn Liniment is
    applied.

153

Clipped from <u>Fisherman and Farmer</u>, <u>29 Jun 1894, Fri</u>, <u>First Edition</u>, <u>Page 2</u>

Mr. H. W. Melvin, ex-teacher of our public school, has been with us during the past ten days, He is a jolly Virginian, and his friends regret his departure.

Mrs. Josephine Leary has returned home after an absence of several months, and is making preparations to erect two brick stores on her lot on burnt square.

Rev. C. M. Cartwright has just returned from Roper. At that point is one of the finest rural charges in the State. Mr. C. is exceedingly popular and has

Clipped from <u>Fisherman and Farmer</u>, <u>14 May 1897, Fri</u>, <u>First Edition</u>, <u>Page 2</u>

Elizabeth City on a visit to her brother, A. H. Mitchell.

Mr. Edgar C. Rea has accepted the position as book-keeper at the Bank of Edenton.

A colored boy by the name of Boyed, had his foot cut off this week at Branning's mill.

Mrs. E. F. Martin, of Elizabeth City, is visiting her daughter, Mrs. John Wood, at Hayes.

Quite a number of Hertford people came here this week to

154

Politics and Civics

African-American residents of Edenton participated in the bipartisan political arena, by holding a Republican convention, voting, and holding various offices. Nominations were made, and offices filled for positions such as Register of Deeds, Legislature, Coroner, County Commissioner, and Justices of the Peace. They also served as jurors. In the late 1890s there were 70 colored Masonic Lodges in North Carolina. The Odd Fellows was a fraternal organization with a framework that promoted personal and social improvement. The Colored Odd Fellows celebrated their 13th anniversary in 1888, so they had been in existence in Edenton since 1875. The Odd Fellows' creed includes a statement about their beliefs-that "all people-irrespective of creed, race, color, nationality, social status, sex, rank, and station, are brothers and sisters".

Other areas of civic concern centered around the upkeep of the "colored cemetery", which had fallen into disrepair; the building of a larger meeting hall for the John R. Page masonic lodge; and erecting a monument to the colored soldiers of the Civil War.

Clipped from <u>Fisherman and Farmer</u>, <u>02 Mar 1888, Fri</u>, <u>First Edition</u>, <u>Page 5</u>

The Oddfellows (colored) of this place will celebrate their universal of thanksgiving on Sunday next and will turn out in full uniform at 3 o'clock. Preaching will be held at Kedash church by Rev. C. W. Winfield.

Clipped from <u>Fisherman and Farmer</u>, <u>24 Aug 1888, Fri</u>, <u>First Edition</u>, <u>Page 5</u>

On Monday next the colored Odd Fellows of this place will celebrate their 13th Anniversary. Several other Lodges have been invited and a large crowd and a good time expected. Rev. C. W. Winfield, W. W. Blair and Philip McDonald will deliver addresses.

Clipped from <u>Fisherman and Farmer</u>, <u>14 Sep 1888, Fri</u>, <u>First Edition</u>, <u>Page 4</u>

THE BITTER WRANGLE OVER.

Tuesday, at 12 o'clock, the long expected convention of colored people to nominate a Republican County Ticket assembled at the Court House in Edenton. We were there and looked eagerly over the body to see if we could find any variation in the predominant color of the assembly. There was none save that produced by the presence of one white man who looked as lonely, as thoroughly isolated and out of place as it is possible ever to conceive a man. Never did a more thoroughly black assembly meet in Chowan county for any purpose. White Republicans were completely ignored. A white man was put in nomination for Chairman of the convention but he was defeated, almost as quick as you could declare it, by Harkness Gussom. The townships were all represented by colored men save in the one instance just referred to.

Clipped from <u>Fisherman and Farmer</u>, <u>20 Dec 1889, Fri</u>, <u>First Edition</u>, <u>Page 5</u>

CELEBRATION.

Our colored people will celebrate the 27th anniversary of the Emancipation Proclamation in grand style. A grand stand will be erected, corner of Main and King streets, from which orations will be delivered by a number of distinguished speakers. A large number, from other counties, will be present and participate in the observances.

Our Mayor will be requested, by the leading colored men in our midst, to appoint a special police force, on the day of the celebration, to keep order &c. This is a good step in the sight direction We congratulate them upon the exercise of a precaution worthy their good citizenship-

Clipped from Fisherman and Farmer, 17 Oct 1890, Fri, First Edition, Page 5

A negro named Squire Pearson is in jail at Raleigh for committing perjury in order to register. If you will examine the registration books in Edenton you will find perjury committed by some of the negroes here, who are anxion to vote before they become of age, and by some not entitled to a vote.

Clipped from <u>Fisherman and Farmer</u>, <u>27 Nov 1891, Fri</u>, <u>First Edition</u>, <u>Page 4</u>

NOTICE.

—— —

There will be a mass meeting of the Colored Citizens of the town Edenton and county of Chowan, at the Court House on Monday night the 14th of Dec. '91, for the purpose of taking into consideration the celebration of emancipation proclamation that will take place on the 7th day of January '92, by local orders of the Harrell Post No. 42 Edenton, N. C. Let all the Lodges of the town and county be interested, H. B Pettegrew, Quarter Master, Hardy Mixon, E. H. Blount, Commanders.

Clipped from <u>Fisherman and Farmer</u>, <u>18 Dec 1891, Fri</u>, <u>First Edition</u>, <u>Page 5</u>

All matters entrusted to me will be attended to upon strict business rules. By prompt and courteous dealings I hope to merit your confidence.

Yours very truly,
ROBERT J. MITCHELL.

Our colored people will celebrate the 28th anniversary of the Emancipation Proclamation in grand style, January 1st

ANSWER THIS Question
Why do so many people we see around us seem to prefer to suffer and be made miserable by Indigestion, Constipation. Dizziness, Loss of Appetite, Coming up of the food, Yellow Skin, when for 75c

Clipped from <u>Fisherman and Farmer</u>, <u>19 Feb 1892, Fri</u>, <u>First Edition</u>, <u>Page 8</u>

The colored cemetery at the head of Granville street is in a very bad condition. We visited this home of the dead on Sunday last and was made to blush with shame We hope our people will give the matter immediate attention, and those who have friends and loved ones who are sleeping beneath the cold od at this place will see to it that some care is taken with this sacred spot.

Clipped from <u>Fisherman and Farmer</u>, <u>18 Mar 1892, Fri</u>, <u>First Edition</u>, <u>Page 8</u>

Rev C. M. Cartwright arrived here Monday. He speaks in very high terms of the recent call he received from the First Baptist church at Severn, N. C. The Rev is making rapid progress at Roper, N. C.

It will be remembered by our readers that the FISHERMAN & FARMER has been talking about the shameful

Clipped from <u>Fisherman and Farmer</u>, <u>18 Mar 1892, Fri</u>, <u>First Edition</u>, <u>Page 8</u>

(cont'd.)

condition of the colored cemetery for some time. We have written lines week after week urging our people to do something to make this sacred spot, the home of the dead, a place that would, at least, remind us that the loved ones there asleep had not been forgotten but their graves were being watched and cared for by their living friends. It is now with much pleasure we see that our people have aroused from their deadly sleep, their negligence of duty, and are now actively at work upon plans that will put it in good order and a creditable condition.

Clipped from Fisherman and Farmer, 25 Mar 1892, Fri, First Edition, Page 5

Still the good work goes on. Rev S. P. Knight made a fine talk about the cemetery on Sunday evening last. Let everybody help to improve it.

The colored people have done well during the last twenty five years, and they can do better by studying economy and looking to the future.

Clipped from Fisherman and Farmer, 29 Jul 1892, Fri, First Edition, Page 8

John R. Page masonic lodge is contemplate building a large and commodious hall in the near futures The building is to be 35 x 60 ft. with two stories. The corner-stone was laid last Monday, July 25th, by District D. G. M., W. J. Herritage, assisted by John R. Page lodge and visiting brethren. At night an entertainment was given at the Opera House, the proceeds of which will be used toward erecting the Temple.

Mr W. W. Blair, president of the Emancipation celebration, has been requested to hold his position until his successor is elected; also other officers Thus a perfect organization will be kept up for celebrating the first day of every January.

The celebration of the Emancipation Proclamation was in every way an enjoyable occasion. As we failed to collect money enough from the public to defray the expense we applied to the Councilmen to aid us, which was responded to by a donation of $25, for which they have our thanks. May they live long to do good. Philip McDonald.

The people of this community will be called upon in a few days to contribute as largely as each one can afford to help raise money to clear up and fence the colored cemetery. It is your duty, it is my duty, and the duty of every one, whether you expect to be buried in Edenton or not. So save your money, be ready and waiting for the call.

Clipped from **Fisherman and Farmer**, **01 Jun 1894, Fri**, **First Edition**, **Page 2**

Decoration day, May 30th, was duly observed by Harrell Post, No 42, G. A. R. Services were held at Kedesh church, from which the procession proceeded to the cemetery where appropriate exercises were also held and the graves of the dead heroes were beautifully decorated. At night an entertainment was held at the Fair ground.

Clipped from **Fisherman and Farmer**, **22 Jun 1894, Fri**, **First Edition**, **Page 3**

Funds are being raised by Harrell Post, No 42, G. A. R., for the purpose of erecting a suitable monument in this city to the colored soldiers of the late war. The movement is a good one and we hope the public will contribute liberally.

Clipped from Fisherman and Farmer, 09 Aug 1895, Fri, First Edition, Page 3

Colored Odd Fellows.

The Grand Lodge of the G. U. O. O. F. of North Carolina is in session this week in this city. It is an intelligent looking body of colored men and we trust their meeting will prove both pleasant and profitable to them.

Clipped from Fisherman and Farmer, 27 Nov 1896, Fri, First Edition, Page 2

The colored people had a big celebration Tuesday in honor of their recent political victory. It was the largest procession of colored people we have ever seen here, and they deserve much credit for their good behavior. There was perfect order and not an arrest made during the whole day. About three thousand were in the parade that passed on Main street.

Clipped from Fisherman and Farmer, 03 Sep 1897, Fri, First Edition, Page 2

The managers of the colored fair which will be held here next week, are quite busy getting the track, buildings, etc., in good condition. If the weather is favorable there will no doubt be a large attendance.

Religion

The church was and still is, without question, the most important and influential institution in African American life. It continues to serve as a social and community center; but first and foremost, it helps its members grow spiritually. Blacks began to form their own churches almost immediately after emancipation. The first two were Kadesh A.M.E. Zion, organized in 1866, and Pleasant Grove A.M.E. Zion, also organized in 1866. There was an early congregation of black Methodists who worshipped in the Sycamore chapel building on the corner of Oakum and Church Streets. Providence Baptist Church was organized two years later in 1868. St. John the Evangelist Episcopal Church was organized in 1881, and in1895, Gale Street Baptist Church was organized. In 1897, Kadesh moved into its new building, the largest sanctuary in Edenton at the time. The church and the parsonage were built by Hannibal Badham, Sr., whose wife Evelina Williams Badham was a member. Their daughter, Sadie Badham Hawkins played the organ for Kadesh for more than 35 years. In the early 20th century, the Edenton Normal and Industrial School offered classes, and housed students, in buildings behind Kadesh Church.

Preaching, celebrations, weddings, funerals, programs, and concerts were all a part of the life of each of these churches. Members and guests from all over attended any number of regular Sunday services, and extra events.

Clipped from <u>Fisherman and Farmer</u>, <u>02 Sep 1887, Fri</u>, <u>First Edition</u>, <u>Page 1</u>

The revival meeting in the colored Methodist church is still in progress. Tuesday night, by appointment, Rev. J. Wm. Lee preached for the Pastor. A tremendous crowd gathered, filling the church to its utmost capacity. Many unable to get in the house, (all, even the standing room being occupied) were compelled to stand on the outside of the building facing the doors and windows. Mr. Lee was at himself and delivered one of the most affective, sensible sermons we ever heard from him. His argument was full and convincing and brought forth every admissible demonstration of approval. A large number of white people filled the galleries of the building who listened to the discourse with attention marked with interest which, from the begining to the close, was unabating. The meeting continues from night to night. Several colored ministers are present, notable among them is Rev. G. W. Lee, D. D., of Washington, D. C., who, as we have said on former occasions, ranks among the very foremost of his race in our State as a pulpit orator. He is a native Carolinian and like all the rest of his race, who, are to the manor born, he demonstrates qualities of mind and character which, to us at least, appear almost decidedly peculiar.

The protracted meetings of the colored Methodist and Baptist churches closed on Sunday, having been attended with more than usual results. The ordinance of baptism, by immersion, was administered on Sunday to candidates for membership of both denominations. As is usual, on such occasions, a large crowd

D EVERY TUESDAY ANI

. C., Friday, Septemb

was present to witness the impressiv scene and to attest the solemn enlistment of happy souls in the great army of the redeemed.

A MISTAKE.

We regret to record the fact that an unusual amount of sickness has prevailed in Edenton during August an September. When October rolls round we hope for a healthier season.—Albe

173

Clipped from <u>Fisherman and Farmer</u>, <u>28 Sep 1888, Fri</u>, <u>First Edition</u>, <u>Page 5</u>

Dr. J. C. Price, (col.) a distinguished orator, who has lectured in portions of Europe and the United States, will deliver a lecture in Edenton, at the A. M. E. Zion Church, Wednesday, October 10th. He will lecture also in E. City Oct. 9th. See bills.

Clipped from <u>Fisherman and Farmer</u>, <u>17 Jan 1890, Fri</u>, <u>First Edition</u>, <u>Page 1</u>

St. Johns, colored, Episcopal church is a handsome little structure. It was most appropriately decorated for Xmas celebration and service. The minister in charge, Rev. Herritage, is growing more and more popular and will succeed in making himself a felt power for good in our midst.

Clipped from Fisherman and Farmer, 17 Jan 1890, Fri, First Edition, Page 5

At St. John's church, there will be a special sermon by Rev. W. J. Herritage, next Sunday afternoon, at 3 o'clock, to the children of the Sunday school. Parents, and the public generally, are cordially invited.

Clipped from Fisherman and Farmer, 30 Oct 1891, Fri, First Edition, Page 4

Grand Rally at Kedesh Church last Sunday. The services were largely attended all day. The amount paid over by friends and members of the church was $131,33. The Pastor and Trustees extend many thanks to the friends in general for their liberal donations, and especially our white friends who have aided us so much in trying to erect a parsonage for our minister. May God bless you all.

Mr R. Shepard, of Oxford, with five little orphan children gave a very fine concert at Providence Baptist church on the night of the 2nd and raised $15.25; also a concert at Kedesh A. M. E. Zion church and raised $11.19; all for the little orphans. May this good work go forward.

Clipped from Fisherman and Farmer, 07 Apr 1893, Fri, First Edition, Page 8

Easter was appropriately celebrated at the A. M. E. Zion church. At 11 o'clock Rev Collins preached one of his soul stirring sermons which brought forth the scene of the resurrection of Christ vividly before his hearers. At 3:15 the Sabbath school, under the management of Supt. Philip McDonald, assisted by others, presented the finest Easter service we ever witnessed. The music was grand and the floral decorations were beyond all expectation.

Clipped from Fisherman and Farmer, 28 Apr 1893, Fri, First Edition, Page 8

Mrs Ellen Pinkney, a female Evangelist, preached during the protracted meeting at Kedesh church during last week. The church was filled to its utmost capacity every night. Some went there through curiosity, others to hear her pre·ch. it not being customary to see women in the pulpit. But she convinced all who heard her that the Lord can raise up whom He will to preach His everlasting Gospel. May she live long to do battle for the Lord.

Clipped from Fisherman and Farmer, 03 Nov 1893, Fri, First Edition, Page 2

BANQUET AT LOVE AND CHARITY HALL.

The young ladies of the A. M. E. Zion Church of Edenton N. C. will give a grand Banquet at Love and Charity Hall on Tuesday, Wednesday, Thursday, and Friday Evenings, Nov. 7, 8. 9. and 10. for the benefit of the Church. Eleven young ladies and four gentlemen will give a grand treat to the public on Thursday evening by performing the great and most touching play of the Ten Virgins. This play alone is well worth the amount that it will take to pay your way in to the banquet for the four nights. The price of admission is only ten cents for each evening.

Last Sunday was a big day for Kedesh church. Rev. M. P. Hawkins about two months ago organized 12 tribes in his church for the purpose of raising $500, and last Sunday was the day appointed for bringing in the sheaves. Services began at 6 with a prayer meeting. At nine o'clock preaching by the Rev. E. Overton; at 11 o'clock preaching by Rev. J. Frances Lee, of Franklin, Va. At 3 o'clock the church was packed, seats could not be found for the audience. The Pleasant Grove choir were present and conducted the music for this service. Preaching by Rev. Overton. At night the audience was immense; music by the S. S. choir; preaching by Rev. J. Francis Lee. At this service the tribes turned in the grand sum of $533.66,

On Sunday last Children's Day exercises were held at the Providence Baptist Church. They were of a very high order. The music was exquisite. Mr. Melvin read an entertaining as well as instructive paper on the necessity of christian training. It evinced careful preparation and complete mastery of the subject. It was well received and all that heard it were impressed with a deeper sense of their responsibility to God. Mr. J. D. Yarborough, the energetic and progressive Supt., is the right man in the right place. Under his leadership there are no hights too lofty for his Sunday School to ascend.

Clipped from <u>Fisherman and Farmer</u>, <u>05 Nov 1897, Fri</u>, <u>First Edition</u>, <u>Page 2</u>

ing is progressing rapidly, and on the completion of the work, will be one of the neatest church edifices in the city.

The handsome church building being erected on Gale street by the A, M. E. Zion church, is rapidly nearing completion, and is a credit alike to our colored citizens and our town.

The little child of Mr. and Mrs. W. D. Pruden, died at the home of its parents on Monday, after an illness of several days.

Bibliography

Bristol, Douglas Walter, Jr. 2009. *Knights of the Razor-Black Barbers in Slavery and Freedom.* Baltimore, Maryland: The Johns Hopkins University Press.

Butchko, Thomas R. 1992. *Edenton An Architectural Portrait.* Edenton, North Carolina: The Edenton Women's Club and Chowan County Government.

Camp, Louis Van. *Images of America-Edenton and Chowan County, North Carolina.* Charleston, SC: 2011.

Hurt, R. Douglas. [Editor] 2003. *African American Life in the Rural South, 1900-1950.* Columbia, Missouri: University of Missouri Press. 2011

Kenzer, Robert C. 1997. *Enterprising Southerners-Black Economic Success in North Carolina 1865-1915.* Charlottesville, Virginia: University Press of Virginia.

McCutcheon, Mark. 1993. *The Writer's Guide to Everyday Life in the 1800s.* Cincinnati, Ohio: Writer's Digest Books.

.

Internet

Branning Manufacturing Company's Albania and Pembroke Mills. *Fisherman and Farmer.* November 22,1895. https://www.newspapers.com/image/62537703/

"History of Black Midwives." International Center for Traditional Childbearing (ICTC). https://ictcmidwives.org/black-midwives/history-of-black-midwives.

"The polite,but consequential Negro policeman." NYPL Digital collections. https://digitalcollections.nypl.org/items/510d47dd-g563-a3d9-e040-e00a18064a99

Machine Treadle Sewing Machine Sewing 1878. Free Vintage Clipart. Clipartkid.com/machine-shop-cliparts

Evans, Walker (photographer). "A man cultivating a field near Tupelo, MS". "Discrimination by USDA Against Black Farmers Gets Presidential." Rural News and Information. http://www.dailyyonder.com/discrimination-usda-against-black-farmers-gets-presidential/2008/03/04/1098/.

"Women boiling and washing clothes 1870s*"* NWHM Exhibit: A History of Women in Industry. https://www.nwhm.org/online-exhibits/industry/5.htm

"Union army blacksmiths working on a portable forge". https://randolphhistory.wordpress.com/tag/blacksmithing/

"1899 Students in a bricklaying class, Hampton Institute, Hampton, Virginia." https://commons.wikimedia.org/wiki/File:Hampton_Institute_-_bricklaying.jpg

"Newberry County South Carolina. Church. View of [African-American] church in thinly populated areas of Newberry County, South Carolina." https://commons.wikimedia.org/wiki/File:NewberryCounty.

"Dolly Johnson, personal cook to President Benjamin Harrison, in the small White House kitchen, in 1890". https://en.wikipedia.org/wiki/White_House_Executive_Chef

"Raising the Story of Menhaden Fishermen". http://beaufortartist.blogspot.com/p/african-americans-in-beaufort-1995.html

"Gulla/Geechee Cultural Heritage Corridor---Places Reflecting America's Diverse Cultures Explore Their Stories in the National park System: A Discover our Shared Heritage Travel Itinerary." National Parks Service. https://www.nps.gov/nr/travel/cultural_diversity/Gullah_Geechee_Cultural_Heritage_Corridor.html.

Smith, W. Eugene (photographer). (1951). "Nurse Midwife". http://www.washingtonmidwives.org/news-events/midwifery-news.html

Kitsteiner, John. "Tapping the Pine Tree: Plant Resins and Their Uses." http://tcpermaculture.com/site/2014/08/04/tapping-the-pine-tree-plant-resins-and-their-uses/

INDEX

A

Adams, Lewis, 84
Alexander, William, 78
Are__, John, 78
Armstead, David, 6
Asbell, Artist, 9
Askew, William, 83
Austen, John, 83
Austin, Joseph, 83
Autterbridge, Daniel, 83

B

Badham, Albert, 5
Badham, Evalina, 171
Badham, Hannibal, 40, 70, 109, 171, 78
Badham, Hannibal, Jr., 70, 78
Badham, Hester, 33
Badham, Mary, 50
Badham, Miles, 70,78
Badham, Prince A., 33
Badham, Sadie, 171
Banks, Andrew, 86
Banks, Jennetta, 27
Baoran (?), Lucy, 8
Barclay, John, 84
Bazemore, Alfred, 80
Beasely, Josephine, 86
Beasley, Annie, 8
Beasley, Auther, 83

Beasley, Charles, 84
Beasley, Fillis, 8
Beasley, Henry, *xx*
Beasley, Jerry, 28, 84
Beasley, Mary, 6
Beasley, Tony, 26
Beasly, Lucy, 86
Belch, Mills, 9
Bell, Joseph, 83
Bell, Robert, 72
Bembry, Bettie, 86
Bembry, William, 83
Bembry, Wilson, 49
Bembry Quartette, 107, 108, 122, 127
Bembury, Atlas, 83
Bembury, Celia, 33
Bembury, Dora, 83
Bembury, Eliza, 86
Bembury, Lawrence, 60
Benbury, ____, 86
Benbury, Abram, 8
Benbury, Augustus, 9
Benbury, Caine, 9
Benbury, Charles, 9
Benbury, Edward, 5
Benbury, Isaac, 5
Benbury, Lawrence, 8
Benbury, Leon, 9
Benbury, Noah, 40
Benbury, Pilgrim, 74
Benbury, Samuel, 33
Benbury, Samuel, 86
Benbury, Shadrack, 3, 8
Benbury, Thomas, 40

Benbury, William, 80

Benbury, Wilson, 9

Bench, Anthony, 33

Bennett, Arthur, 82

Bennett, Jerry, 60

Benton, Biddy, 4

Benton, Reuben, 6

Bess, Noah, 84

Best, Noah, 27

Birnett, Charity, 9

Bizzell, Joseph, 6

Bizzell, Rufus, 77

Bizzell, Venus, 27

Black Diamond Quartette, 126

Blair, Charles, 22

Blair, Clarissa, 33

Blair, Elijah, 56

Blair, Henderson, 8, 56

Blair, John, 86

Blair, Jordan, 40

Blair, Joseph, 60

Blair, Mary, 33

Blair, Penelope, 8

Blair, W.W., 156, 166

Blanchard, Edward, 40

Blanchard, John, 6

Blount, _____, 83

Blount, Alfred, 41

Blount, Allen, 8

Blount, Alley, 8

Blount, Anthony, 5

Blount, Charles, 9

Blount, David, 22,49

Blount, Edward, 40, 49

Blount, Eliza, 8, 33

Blount, George, 5

Blount, Henry, 8

Blount, Isaac, 82

Blount, James, 5

Blount, John, 4, 86

Blount, Joseph B., 35

Blount, Maxwell, 9

Blount, Mills, 6

Blount, Nelson, 60

Blount, Thancy, 6

Blount, Virgil, 9

Blount, William, 9

Blunt, Hannibal, 74

Blunt, Henry, 84

Blunt, Robert, 83

Bond, Anthony, 6, 60

Bond, Augustus, 3

Bond, Charles, 33

Bond, Dave, 83

Bond, David, 4

Bond, E_____, 84

Bond, Fr_____, 74

Bond, Gaston, 4

Bond, George, 6

Bond, H_____, 78

Bond, Harry, 4

Bond, Henry, 3

Bond, Joe, 4

Bond, John, 4

Bond, Joseph, 4

Bond, Major, 4

Bond, Norfleet, 83

Bond, Rose, 4

Bond, Sarah, 27
Bond, Thomas, 3
Bond, William, 83
Bond, Willis, 6
Bonner, _____, 4
Bonner, Author, 42
Bonner, Mike, 83
Bookman, Sydney, 41
Boon, William, 80
Bosley, John, 9
Boston, Albert, 83
Boston, Charles, 121
Bownes, Fred, 72
Boyed, _____, 154
Bradley, Thomas, 83
Brady, Stephen, 9
Brewer, Henry, 49
Bricks, Luke, 5
Bright, _____, 78
Bright, William, 78
Brinkley, Henry, 80
Brinkley, James, 26
Brown, Delia, 33
Brown, Easter, 5
Brown, Marko, 4
Brown, Matthew, 83
Brown, William, 6
Brownrigg, Fred, 3
Bryant, _____, 83
Bullock, Major, 4
Bullock, Moses, 6
Bunch, A_____, 72
Bunch, Samuel, 8
Bunche, Franke, 4

Burden, Ira, 83
Burk, Moses, 80
Burke, Major, 6
Burke, Maria, 84
Burke, Penelope, 46
Burke, Susan, 84
Burke, William, 72
Burt, Frank, 72
Burton, S.J., 119
Butts, Elijah, 83

C

Cabarrus, Noah, 6
Cabarrus, Pulliam 6
Cabarrus, Tob, 136
Cabarrus, Tom, 136
Cabarrus, Truman, 6
Cambrell, Thomas, 6
Capehart, John, 84, 99
Capehart, Paul, 84
Capeheart, William, 83
Carter, George, 40, 83
Caskie, R.A., 44
Charleston, Job, 17,33
Charlton, Annie, 27
Charlton, Edward, 35, 78
Charlton, Job, 17, 35, 40
Charlton, Joseph, 85
Cheshire, Frank, 22
Cheshire, Hester, 33
Cheshire, Lucy, 27
Cheshire, Thomas, 27, 81
Churden, Theodore, 33
Clark, James, 5

Ellis, William, 73
Eppes, Ransom, 27
Epps, Robert, 80
Eure, Steven, 72

F

Farand, Mary, 9
Faribault, Chloe, 27
Faribault, Prince A., 27
Faton(?), John, 4
Felton, Chloe, 9
Felton, John, 93, 94
Felton, Jonah, 8
Felton, Martin, 86
Felton, Pleasant, 27
Felton, Richard, 8
Felton, Spence(r), 104, 105, 106
Felton, Tim, 72
Ferribo, Richard, 83
Fisher, Barral, 83
Fleetwood, Fn?agh, 5
Foxwell, Alfred, 3
Foxwell, Ned, 83
Freeman, Edward, 78
Freeman, William, 9
Frieman, General, 72
Fry, Robert, 9
Furman, Arthur, 9

G

Gatlin, Joseph, 84
Gatling, Joseph, 35
Gatling, Silvey, 6
Gilbert, Rose, 6

Gilford, Eli, 80
Gilliam, Amie, 6, 7
Gilliam, Atlas, *xix*, 60
Gilliam, Henry, 9, 83
Gilliam, Peterson, 5
Gilliam, Sallie, 27
Gilliam, Thomas, 83
Gilliam, Thompson, 5
Goodwin, Elijah, 27
Goodwin, James, 78
Goodwin, Julia, 33
Goodwin, Miles, 9
Goodwin, Stephen, 3
Gordon, Ca___, 83
Gordon, Sophelia, 33
Gorham, Annie, 33
Granberry, Harrison, 9
Granby, Walter, 86
Green, A___, 80
Gregory, Abraham, 78
Gregory, Austin, 26
Gregory, Charles, 9
Gregory, Harry, 3
Gregory, Henry, 80
Gregory, James, 60
Gregory, John, 26
Gregory, Joseph, 27
Gregory, Silvia, 27
Gregory, Wilson, 6
Grice, Anthony, 26
Griffin, Mozella, 28
Gussom, Christiana, 8
Gussom, Harkness, 157

H

H_____, Taylor, 83
Halsey, James, 80
Harden, George, 81
Harding, G_____, 81
Harding, Joseph, 72
Harrell, Annie, 33
Harrell, M_____, 86
Harrell, S_____, 72
Harris, Sadie, 84
Harriss, William, 81
Hart, Richard, 79
Harvey, Osborne, 33
Hassell, Warren, 83
Hathaway, _____, 83
Hathaway, Elijah, 40
Hathaway, Mose, 83
Haughton, Emily, 56
Haughton, Jeffrey, 27
Haughton, Mary, 26
Haughton, Melvina, 27
Hawkins, Thomas, 82
Heath, William, 40
Heritage, William, 79
Hill, Caroline, 26
Hobbs, Hester, 84
Holley, Edward, 74
Holley, L_____, 86
Holley, Masoniah, 83
Hollowell, W___, 72
Horton, Ch_____, 86
Horton, G_____, 81
Horton, Jeffrey, 72
Horton, Solomon, 86

Howard, _____, 81
Hyman, Matilda, 27

I

Iredell, Aaron, 40
Iredell, Henry, 35, 77

J

Jackson, John, 3
James, Ella, 86
James, Henry, 35, 135
James, Henry, *xx*, 36, 37, 38, 135
James, Primus, 83
Jeanes(?), Henry, 77
Jerkins, Richard, 6, 49
Johnson, Aaron, 3
Johnson, Alfred, 4
Johnson, Allen, 3
Johnson, Anthony, 6
Johnson, D., 4
Johnson, David/Daniel, 3
Johnson, Isaac, 84
Johnson, James, 83
Johnson, John, 3
Johnson, Lunon, 8
Johnson, Mack, 3
Johnson, Marcella, 9
Johnson, Mary, 56
Johnson, Primus, 6
Johnson, Thomas, 83
Johnson, Wills, 6
Johnston, Allen, 78
Johnston, Caroline, 26
Johnston, Giah, 26

Johnston, Henry, 40

Johnston, Hester, 27

Johnston, London, 27

Johnston, Malcolm, 78,80

Johnston, Nathaniel, 83

Johnston, Rufus, 33

Johnston, Sarah, 33

Johnston, Theodore, 85

Johnston, Wells, 26

Jones, America, 3

Jones, Benbury, 72

Jones, Charles, 40

Jones, Frederick, 83

Jones, Gilbert, 83

Jones, James, 34, 73, 93

Jones, James, 73

Jones, M_____, 86

Jones, Ma_____, 78

Jones, Martha, 6, 84

Jones, Mary, 27

Jones, Nellie, 116

Jones, Peter, 20

Jones, Vandon, *xx*, 75

Jones, Walter, 60

Jones, William, 4, 8

Jordan, David, 78

Jordan, Elijah, 40

Jordan, Elijah, Jr. 40

Jordan, Ellen, 33

Jordan, Henry, 5

Jordan, Joseph, 8

Jordan, Mary, 86

Jordan, Samuel, 40

Jordan, Samuel, 6

Jordan, Susan, 42

Jordan, Wesley, 5

K

Kale, John, 49

Kane, Peter, 4

Kellam, Jacob, 26

Kelley, Joseph, 85

King, Alfred, 40

King, Henry, 26

King, Jim (James), 93, 94

King, John, 17

King, Nancy, 84

King, Peter, 40

Kinnell, Augustus, 60

Knight, Rev. Simon/Simond P., *xx*, 1, 79, 101, 146, 165

L

Lamb, John, 6

Lane, George, 57, 109

Lane, Luch, 57, 109

Lassiter, ___J___, 72

Latham, Alexander, 81

Latham, Millicent, 33

Launner, Thomas, 4

Lawrence, Thomas, 5

Leary, Ephram A., Jr., 9

Leary, Jerry, 4

Leary, Josephine, 133, 154

Leary, Robert, 9

Leary, Spencer, 4

Leary, Sweety, *xx*, 34, 93, 133

Leary, Thomas, 9

Mins, Edgar, 84
Mitchell, Catherine, 5
Mitchell, Dorson, 83
Mixon, Hardy, 33
Moon, Margaret, 6
Moore, Andrew, 86
Moore, Jim, 96
Moore, Lillie, 86
Moore, Louisa, 5
Moore, Lu___ 84
Morris, David, 4
Morris, Hester, 72
Murdough, David, 27
Murphy, _____, 78
Muse, Nathaniel, 27

N

Nelson, Thomas, 83
Newbern, Leroy, 45
Newbern, Miles, 4
Nichols, Henry, 78
Nixon, Arthur, 8
Nixon, Charity, 6, 27
Nixon, Della, 8
Nixon, Edmund, 58
Nixon, Henry, 83
Nixon, Isaac, 27
Nixon, James, 5
Nixon, Margaret, 6
Nixon, Mary, 27, 86
Nixon, Moses, 9
Nixon, Squire, 3
Nixon, Thomas, 9
Nixon, William, 33

Norcom, John, 35
Norcon/Norcum, Carolina, 27
Norcum, Edward, 9
Norcum, John, 83
Norcum, Julia, 9

O

Orange, John, 9
Osten, Gregory, 9
Outlaw, Edy, 27
Outlaw, James, 72
Overton, _____, 79
Overton, Billy, 97, 98
Overton, Charlotte, 6, 51
Overton, Henrietta, 86
Overton, Kate, 6
Overton, Nathan, 40
Overton, Rev. E., 180
Owens, Daniel, 78
Owens, Isaac, 8, 78
Owens, Solomon, 60, 77

P

Page, Hartkis, 8
Page, Jane, 27
Page, John R., 78
Page, John T., 40
Page, Laura, 26
Page, Lonan, 6
Page, Mollie, 86
Page, Nathan, 9
Pailin, _____, 83
Pain, Almeta, 86
Pain, Att___, 86

Parker, Moses, 5

Parrish, Sandy, 5

Paxton, Abram, 41

Paxton, Abram, 5, 6

Paxton, Charity, 27, 86

Paxton, Charles, 6, 26

Paxton, David, 8, 56, 74

Paxton, Dink, 149

Paxton, Edward, 84

Paxton, Fannie, 27

Paxton, Henry 60

Paxton, James, 8, 78, 83

Paxton, Jane, 33

Paxton, Jenny, 33

Paxton, John, 6

Paxton, Joseph, 8

Paxton, Miles, 40

Paxton, Nat, 6

Paxton, Robert, 5

Paxton, Thomas, 60, 72, 74

Paxton, William, 83

Pearson, Squire, 159

Peat, Edward, 83

Perkins, Atlas, 5

Perkins, Grace, 8

Perkins, Isaac, 8

Perkins, Major, 6, 60, 74

Perry, Catherine, 33

Perry, Go___, 74

Perry, Martin, 72

Perry, Walisous, 83

Petigrew, Anthony, 5

Petigrew, Haywood, 79

Phelps, Mi___, 81

Picier(?), Mingo, 9

Picke, MaryJane, 9

Picott, Annie, 27

Picott, Horace, 56

Pierce, Sherman, 26

Pinkney, Ellen, 178

Pot(?), Patience, 6

Powell, Henry, 78

Powell, James, 72

Price, Dr. J.C., 174

Price, James, 4,49

Price, Jane, 86

Price, Joseph, 40, 70

Pruden, Thomas, 26, 78

Q

Quickstep Brass Band, 130, 131, 132

R

R_____, Alexander, 83

Ransom, George, 9

Reaves, S_____, 73

Reddick, Langston, 6

Reddick, Samuel, 49

Reed, Gorge, 83

Reed, Rial/Rijas, *xx*, 60, 64

Reed, Van, 83

Reeves, Frank, 81

Reid, James, 83

Rhodes, Daniel, 4

Ria, James, 9

Riddick, Elliott, 86

Riddick, Richard, 79

Riddick, Sampson, 17
Right, Stephen, 3
Roberts, Armstead, 9
Roberts, Glasgow, 6, 27
Roberts, Haywood, 9
Roberts, Nelly, 6, 33
Robins, Comfort, 6
Robinson, Joseph, 9
Rogers, Henry, 78
Rollings, John, 72
Roman, Lewis, 83
Ruci(?), James, 3
Rumbolt, John, 3
Rumbough, Abram, 27
Rumbough, Horace, 60
Rumbough, Mathias, 33
Runnels, Hamilton, 8
Ryan, No___, 86
Ryan, Pattie, 26
Ryan, Sally, 8
Ryan, Thadius, 5
Ryan, W., 101

S

Sanders, Riddick, 138
Satterfield, Isaac, 4
Satterfield, M.J., 101
Satterfield, Richard, 83
Satterfield, Thomas, 83
Satterfield, Tredwell, 3
Saunders, _____, 83
Saunders, Mike, 6
Sawyer, Annie, 84
Sawyer, Betsey, 148

Sawyer, Dinah, 6
Sawyer, Henry, 81
Sawyer, James, *xx*, 75, 76
Sawyer, John, 6
Sawyer, Zall, 26
Sawyer, Zel, 8
Sells, Thomas, 9
Shannonhouse, Alfonso, 6
Shapp, Sha___sty, 83
Sharp, Abram, 9
Shears, John, 72
Shepard, R. 176
Sherton, John, 83
Silves, Elbert, 83
Simpkins, Samuel, 59
Simpson, Arter, 9
Simpson, Nelson, 6
Simpson, Richard, 6
Simpson, Susan, 33
Sivells, Larry, 72
Skank, Jennie, 106
Skinner, Andrew, 5
Skinner, Anthony, 60
Skinner, Arnato/Arnold, 3
Skinner, Augustus, 9
Skinner, C.S., Jr., 140
Skinner, Caroline, 5
Skinner, Charles, 72
Skinner, Cora, 84
Skinner, Daniel, 4
Skinner, E.D., 149
Skinner, Edy, 33
Skinner, Fannie, 50
Skinner, Fred, 9

Skinner, George, Sr., 40

Skinner, Harry, 9

Skinner, Henry, 4

Skinner, Jacob, *xix,* 27, 32, 140

Skinner, James, 5, 6

Skinner, Jane, 27

Skinner, John L., 35

Skinner, John, 5, 8, 77

Skinner, Joseph, 40

Skinner, L_____, 81

Skinner, M_____, 73

Skinner, Martha, 86

Skinner, Moses, 8, 39

Skinner, Nelly, 6

Skinner, Nelson, 6,

Skinner, Perry, 5

Skinner, Peter, 6, 33

Skinner, Simon, 4

Skinner, Stant/Staut, 39

Skinner, Treecy/Tracy, 27

Skinner, Violet, 33

Skinner, W.F., 148

Skinner, Warren, 45

Small, Abigail, 8

Small, Mills, 9

Small, Thomas, 8

Smith, Cambridge, 3

Smith, David, 27

Smith, G___, 83

Smith, George, 27

Smith, Harrison, 6

Smith, Larken/Larkin, 17, 35

Smith, Mary, 56

Snowden, Isaac, 6

Spellman, Dagmon/Damon, 60

Spencer, John, 4

Sprout, Maggie, 86

Spruil, E___, 83

Spruill, Charles, 86

Spruill, Gilbert, 72, 84

Stallings, Augustus, 84

Stallings, Ostin, 5

Stallings, Washington, 5

Stallings, William, 5

Standing, George, 5

Standing, Mack, 8

Steward, Isam, 23

Steward, Isiah, 8

Steward/Stewart, Dorsey, 23, 51

Stewart, Isiah, 40

Sturgis, William, 52

Sutton, Anderson, 6

Sutton, Edward, *xix,* 27, 28

Sutton, Jonas, 8

Sutton, Ransom, 5

Sutton, Susan, 27

Swan, Thomas, 6

T

Tatem/Tatum, Miles, 40, 78

Taylor, _____, 83

Taylor, Isaac, 9

Taylor, John, 121

Taylor, Joseph, 9

Taylor, Sheridan, 86

Thatch, Cherry, 6

Thatchell, William, 83

Thomas, Martha, 27

Tillery, Lewis/Louis, *xx*, 35, 36, 37, 38, 84

Treadwell, Frank, 3

Tredwill, M____, 84

Trip, Robert, 8

Trotman, Ham, 5

Turner, Florence, 33

Turner, Tamer, 33

Tyler, John, 78

U

Underhill, Nancy, 86

Underhill, Nelson, 26

V

Valentine, Alexander, 4

Vaughn, Jonas, 8

W

Waff, Frank, 5

Waff, George, 5

Waff, Martha, 6

Waff, Thomas, 8

Walker, Francis, 74

Walters, Mary, 5

Ward, Daniel, 4

Warden, Margaret, 4

Warner, Charity, 4

Warren, Austin, 4

Warren, Hardy, 4

Warren, Primus, 4

Welch, Robert, 4

West, T.S., 134

West, William, 83

Whedbee, Hester, 33

Whedbee, James, 33

Whedbee, Jenny, 27

Whedbee, Louisa, 27

Whidbee, Albert, 8

Whidbee, Edward, 4

Whidbee, Simeon, 4

Whidbee, Willis, 78

White, Alexander, 83

White, Harriet, 27

White, Jerry, 9

White, John, 74

White, Lewis, 4

White, Pennie, 86

White, Samuel, 80

White, Virgil, 3

Whitford, ____, 84

Whitley, Nancy, 8, 26

Wiggins, L., 4

Wilder, Boston, 8, 27

Wilder, Charles, 4

Wilder, Mike, 4

Wilder, Thomas, 4

Wilder, Walter, 27

Wilder, William, 33

Wilkins, Ann, 27

Wilkins, John, 4

Williams, Ava, 86

Williams, Charles, 3

Williams, Evalina, 109

Williams, George, 5, 33

Williams, Hannah, 84

Williams, Hattie, 84

Williams, Henrietta, 77

Williams, John, 20

Williams, Lucinda, 86

Williams, Mary, 86

Williams, Milly, 51

Williams, Octavious, 34, 93

Williams, Philip, 27

Wills, Jacob, 9

Wills, John, 6

Wills, Thomas, 6

Wilson, Cornelius, 6

Wilson, Robert, 8

Wilson, Smith, 26

Wilson, Stephen, 9

Windfield, Silas, 79

Winfield, Rev. C.W., 156

Winn, Fred, 4

Wise, Henry, 121

Woddard, Jennie, 21

Wood, John, 79

Woodley, Llewellyn, 26

Wright, Gregory, 4

Wright, Harry/Harvey, 9

Wright, Reuben, 23

Wright, Sarah, 4

Wrighton, Mack, 9

Wrighton, Miles, 6

Wyn, Betsy, 86

Wynn, Adline, 74

Wynn, Alexander, 3

Wynn, Rev. Blount, 145, 146

Wynn, Richard, 8, 60, 86

Wynn, Thomas, 60

Y

Yarborough, J.D., 181

Yarbrough, Jeff, 83

"A river who forgets its own source will dry up."

...Yoruban proverb